US Foreign Policy sin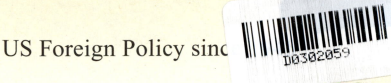

US Foreign Policy since 1945 is an essential and concise introduction to postwar US foreign policy. This book explores the key questions of who makes policy, why, in what style or tradition, under what kinds of democratic controls and in what kind of international environment.

US Foreign Policy since 1945 provides challenging and thought-provoking analysis of the crucial issues, including:

- containment
- Presidential war powers
- realism and idealism
- the Cuban missile crisis
- Vietnam, Panama, Yugoslavia and Kosovo
- the New World Order
- US interventionism and exit strategies

Alan P. Dobson is Professor of Politics at the University of Dundee and his books include *Anglo-American Relations in the Twentieth Century* (Routledge, 1995) and *Deconstructing and Reconstructing the Cold War* (Ashgate, 1999). **Steve Marsh** is a Jean Monnet Lecturer at the University of Cardiff and is currently working on several publications on Anglo–American relations and EU external relations.

The Making of the Contemporary World
Edited by Eric Evans and Ruth Henig
University of Lancaster

The Making of the Contemporary World series provides challenging interpretations of contemporary issues and debates within strongly defined historical frameworks. The range of the series is global, with each volume drawing together material from a range of disciplines – including economics, politics and sociology. The books in this series present compact, indispensable introductions for students studying the modern world.

Titles include:

The Uniting of Europe
From discord to concord
Stanley Henig

International Economy since 1945
Sidney Pollard

United Nations in the Contemporary World
David J. Whittaker

Latin America
John Ward

Thatcher and Thatcherism
Eric J. Evans

Decolonization
Raymond Betts

The Soviet Union in World Politics, 1945–1991
Geoffrey Roberts

China Under Communism
Alan Lawrance

The Cold War
An interdisciplinary history
David Painter

Conflict and Reconciliation in the Contemporary World
David J. Whittaker

States and Nationalism
Malcolm Anderson

Dividing and Uniting Germany
J.K.A. Thomeneck and Bill Niven

Forthcoming titles include:

Multinationals
Peter Wardley

Pacific Asia
Yumei Zhang

**Conflicts in the Middle East
since 1945**
*Beverley Milton-Edwards and
Peter Hinchcliffe*

The Irish Question
Patrick Maume

Right-Wing Extremism
Paul Hainsworth

**Women and Political Power in
Europe since 1945**
Ruth Henig and Simon Henig

US Foreign Policy since 1945

Alan P. Dobson and Steve Marsh

Routledge
Taylor & Francis Group

LONDON AND NEW YORK

First published 2001
by Routledge
11 New Fetter Lane, London EC4P 4EE

Simultaneously published in the USA and Canada by
Routledge
29 West 35th Street, New York, NY 10001

Reprinted 2003

Routledge is an imprint of the Taylor & Francis Group

© 2001 Alan P. Dobson and Steve Marsh

Typeset in Times New Roman by Bookcraft Ltd, Stroud
Printed and bound in Great Britain by TJ International Ltd,
Padstow, Cornwall

British Library Cataloguing in Publication Data
A catalogue record for this book is available from the British
Library

Library of Congress Cataloging in Publication Data
Dobson, Alan P.
   US foreign policy since 1945/Alan P. Dobson and Steve
Marsh
      p. cm. -- (The making of the contemporary world)
   Includes bibliographical references and index.
   ISBN 0–415–24055–7 – ISBN 0–415–17293–4 (pbk)
   1. United States–Foreign relations–1945–1989. 2. United
States–Foreign relations–1989– I. Title: United States
foreign policy since 1945. II. Title: U.S. foreign policy since
1945. III. Marsh, Steve, 1967– IV. Title. V. Series.
E744.D557 2000
327.73–dc21   00–036897

ISBN 0–415–24055–7 (hbk)
ISBN 0–415–17293–4 (pbk)

To my teachers who made the greatest difference – Geoffrey G. Flitton, David J. Manning and Charles Reynolds.

Alan Dobson

To my family and Nuria, and in memory of Miguel – who in 1999 lost too young the greatest right of all.

Steve Marsh

Contents

Abbreviations and acronyms   xi
Key personnel   xiii
Preface   xv

1 US foreign policy: evolution, formulation and execution   1

2 The US and the Cold War: explanation and early
   containment, 1945–61   18

3 Superpower collaboration and confrontation: US
   containment policy, 1961–91   30

4 Economic statecraft   46

5 The US and Europe, 1950–89: beware your allies?   56

6 Hegemony and the Western Hemisphere   65

7 The US and Asia, 1945–89   76

8 The US, Africa and the Middle East, 1945–89   91

9 The US and the post-Cold War disorder   104

10 Contemporary challenges   124

Notes   139
Further reading   147
Index   153

Abbreviations and acronyms

ABMs	Anti-ballistic missile system
APEC	Asian Pacific Economic Co-operation
ASEAN	Association of South East Asian Nations
CAP	Common Agricultural Policy
CEEC	Central and East European Countries
CENTO	Central European Treaty Organisation
CFE	Conventional Forces in Europe
CFSP	Common Foreign and Security Policy
CIA	Central Intelligence Agency
CJTF	Combined Joint Task Forces
EC	European Community
EDC	European Defence Community
ESDI	European Security and Defence Identity
EU	European Union
EXCOM	Executive Committee of the National Security Council
GATT	General Agreement on Tariffs and Trade
GDP	Gross Domestic Product
GNP	Gross National Product
ICBMs	Intercontinental ballistic missiles
IMF	International Monetary Fund
INF	Intermediate Nuclear Force
ITO	International Trade Organisation
MAD	Mutual Assured Destruction
MFN	Most Favoured Nation
MLNF	Multilateral Nuclear Force
MNCs	Multinational corporations
MRBM	Medium Range Ballistic Missiles
NAFTA	North American Free Trade Agreement
NATO	North Atlantic Treaty Organisation
NEC	National Economic Council

NSA	National Security Adviser
NSC	National Security Council
OAS	Organisation of American States
OPEC	Organisation of Petroleum Exporting Countries
PRC	People's Republic of China
UFC	United Fruit Company
UNPROFOR	United Nations Protection Force
SALT	Strategic Arms Limitation Talks
SDI	Strategic Defence Initiative
SEATO	South East Asia Treaty Organisation
START	Strategic Arms Reduction Talks
UN	United Nations
US	United States of America
USAID	US Agency for International Development
USACDA	US Arms Control and Disarmament Agency
USIA	US Information Agency
USSR	Union of Soviet Socialist Republics
USTR	US Trade Representative
VERs	Voluntary export restraint (agreements)
VIEs	Voluntary import expansion (targets)
WEU	Western European Union
WTO	World Trade Organisation

Key personnel

PRESIDENTS

Harry S. Truman	1945–53
Dwight D. Eisenhower	1953–61
John F. Kennedy	1961–63
Lyndon B. Johnson	1963–69
Richard M. Nixon	1969–74
Gerald R. Ford	1974–77
James E. Carter	1977–81
Ronald R. Reagan	1981–89
George H.W. Bush	1989–93
William J. Clinton	1993–

SECRETARIES OF STATE

James F. Byrnes	1945–47
George C. Marshall	1947–49
Dean Acheson	1949–53
John Foster Dulles	1953–59
Christian A. Herter	1959–61
Dean Rusk	1961–69
William P. Rogers	1969–73
Henry A. Kissinger	1973–77
Cyrus R. Vance	1977–80
Edmund S. Muskie	1980–81
Alexander M. Haig Jr.	1981–82
George P. Schultz	1982–89
James A. Baker III	1989–92
Lawrence Eagleburger	1992–93
Warren W. Christopher	1993–95
Madeleine Albright	1995–

Sidney W. Souers	1947–50
James S. Lay Jr.	1950–53
Robert Cutler	1953–55
Dillon Anderson	1955–56
William A. Jackson	1956
Robert Cutler	1957–58
Gordon Gray	1958–61
McGeorge Bundy	1961–66
Walt W. Rostow	1966–69
Henry A. Kissinger	1969–75
Brent Scowcroft	1975–77
Zbigniew Brzezinski	1977–81
Richard V. Allen	1981
William P. Clark Jr.	1981–83
Robert C. McFarlane	1983–85
John M. Poindexter	1985–86
Frank C. Carlucci	1986–87
Colin L. Powell	1987–89
Brent Scowcroft	1989–93
Anthony Lake	1993–95
Samuel Berger	1995–

Preface

In a work like this the most difficult conundrum is always what to leave out. We found the decisions difficult and the outcome not always entirely satisfactory. Nevertheless, our remit was to provide a concise, yet broad, overview of post-war US foreign policy and make our readers think. We have thus pursued a delicate balance between providing sufficient information for readers to formulate their independent judgements about US foreign policy issues and providing our own, or renderings of other people's, interpretations and judgements. We think that the proportions meet the requirements of the book's general recipe.

Like any authors, we hope the reader will pick this book up and be unable to put it down before reaching the final page. It is designed to provide a coherent account of how US foreign policy started out in 1945, how it developed and engaged with a bewildering range of challenges, and how it ended up at the close of the millennium. It also introduces the reader to some perennial problems of US foreign policy-making, to some stimulating theories and interpretations of both US foreign policy and international relations in general, and to some of the ethical problems which afflict this most spacious of all public realms of decision-making.

However, the book has been structured and written in such a way that readers can also 'pick and mix' chapters in response to their interests and needs. Unlike many other works on post-war US foreign policy it is not just a chronological account. There are analytical chapters, such as Chapters 1 and 10, strongly chronological chapters such as Chapters 2, 3, and 9, and a series of chapters that deal with US regional policies in Europe, the Western Hemisphere, the Middle East and Africa, and Asia. We would recommend that Chapter 1 is a necessary pre-requisite for everything that follows. Thereafter it is possible to select themes, such as the Cold War (Chapters 2 and 3), or economic aspects of foreign policy (Chapter 4), or any of the regionally structured chapters, such as Asia in Chapter 7.

Finally, this has been a co-operative effort in the fullest, and the best, sense of the term. When we set out, we each took primary responsibility for designated chapters. However, after draft, re-draft, and detailed discussion, the more libellous conclusions were prudently deleted, and claims to sole authorship of any chapter were lost amid the edited cuttings and the merging of chapters. Above all else, we hope two things. First, that the reader enjoys this as much as we enjoyed writing it. Second, that it does the job: imparts some understanding of US foreign policy, discomforts cosy preconceptions about the impact of the US upon the world, and encourages our audience to delve deeper into the challenging and sometimes murky realm of post-war American foreign policy.

Alan P. Dobson and Steve Marsh
28 January 2000

1 US foreign policy

Evolution, formulation and execution

President Clinton and I ... have spoken often about the goals of American foreign policy. Boiled down, these have not changed in more than 200 years. They are to ensure the continued security, prosperity, and freedom of our people.

Madeleine Albright, US Secretary of State, 1998[1]

Such words provoke more questions than they answer. Under conditions of post-Cold War globalisation, concepts such as security, prosperity and freedom differ in meaning from what they meant in even the recent past. And what exactly is foreign policy? This is not the fatuous question it may seem. Traditionally, the answer has been the pursuit of the national interest in the external relations of states. But there has never been a precise boundary between the domestic and international spheres and the increasing permeability of the state has created a burgeoning of intermestic issues. Furthermore, scholars have long recognised that national interests change, even though they are always concerned with economic well-being, political values and security. The US national interest is never an uncontested set of objectives, and increasingly it has to take into account non-state actors and organisations such as the United Nations (UN), the European Union (EU), the North American Free Trade Agreement (NAFTA), and multinational corporations (MNCs), which play according to international or supranational rather than national rules.

Even when the focus falls on the state, analysing how it acts is difficult. Scholars used to simplify things by assuming that states made rational decisions in the pursuit of objective national interests. More recently, less rational processes have been emphasised by which political constituencies and bureaucracies mediate perceptions of interests and thus influence and often determine foreign policy outcomes. There is also tension between the respective needs of democracy and those of foreign policy-making. There may not be time for democratic procedures in a Cuban missile crisis. At a more purely ethical level, are all means justified to secure the national interest? Might not some means corrupt the democratic state that they are supposed to preserve?[2]

Fuller and nuanced explanations of how US foreign policy-makers resolve tensions between democratic values and state needs, and how they define the national interest and implement foreign policy in a highly complex and changing environment, will come later. All that is offered here is a crude template to identify the analytical challenges involved in foreign policy studies.

The next questions are more specific. Who makes US foreign policy, in accordance with what principles, and with what objectives? To answer these questions adequately, we need to develop a detailed picture of both the ancestry and more recent progeny of US foreign policy. John Dos Passos in *Manhattan Transfer* made his characters strive to discover 'the heart of things'. This book aims to do the same with US foreign policy. However, as Dos Passos' characters found, the 'heart' is often elusive or is determined by the eye of the beholder. Let us start by examining some of the arteries that feed into the heart of US foreign policy.

Exceptionalism

The US was conceived of by the Founding Fathers as a nation with a mission to propagate a special form of political morality, often referred to as exceptionalism. Like other spawn of revolution, Americans brought something different to government. Humanity was conceived of in terms of rights to life, liberty, and the pursuit of happiness, and Enlightenment rationalism concluded that a form of government had to be devised to protect those rights. This was done by controlling political power with a written constitution and a bill of rights and by creating a system of checks and balances, between the federal executive, legislature and judiciary, between the Senate and the House of Representatives in the Congress, and between federal and state sovereignty. Further safeguards were due process of law and popular elections. The result was perceived as something unique and superior to political experience in the Old World. Abraham Lincoln described it as government of the people, by the people, for the people, where people were defined as rights-carrying individuals.

This was a society committed in principle to justice and freedom for all. It was an ambitious, moral enterprise and its values were cast in universal language, which referred to all humanity, not just Americans. However, while domestic policy-making was set in a carefully ordered political environment, which enjoyed a working consensus of values (at least for the most part), the field of foreign policy was different. It was not easy to abide by democratic principles in a realm bereft of anything comparable to domestic law and lacking a body capable of enforcing rules of conduct. The international sphere was characterised by anarchy, self-help and power politics, where survival was the overriding priority and other states subscribed to different codes of political morality. This posed problems. In the mid-1970s, President Carter spoke of human rights as absolute principles, but then discovered that overriding needs for national security transformed absolutes into relative moral values. For example, Iran was such an important ally in the cosmic struggle with communism that its appalling human rights record had to be tolerated. Similarly, with regard both to the persecution of Soviet dissidents like Anatoly Shcharansky and restrictions on Jewish emigration from the Soviet Union, Carter had to tone down criticisms for the sake of important advances with the Soviets on national security matters such as the Strategic Arms Limitation Talks II (SALT II). These issues thus raise important questions. To what extent could the US conduct a principled democratic foreign policy? And how far should it go in trying to spread its universalist values abroad?

Isolationism and internationalism

Pride in its society and government produced two incompatible styles of foreign policy, both of which tried to cope with the problem of America's universalism in an anarchic state system. The first was isolationism, which aimed to protect the new republic's integrity by avoiding entanglement in European conflicts because European states, until the twentieth century, were more powerful than the US and because they fought according to the rules of amoral power politics, which elevated state interests and survival above everything else. The second inclination was to spread liberty abroad, to pursue US economic interests, and, in the twentieth century, to seek security through a world reformed in accordance with US principles. This was internationalism.

In the eighteenth and nineteenth centuries these two approaches to policy vied with each other. President Washington in his farewell address cautioned that 'it must be unwise in us to implicate ourselves by artificial ties in the ordinary vicissitudes of her [Europe's] politics or the ordinary combinations and collisions of her friendships and enmities.'[3] Extend America's commercial activities by all means, but keep out of Europe's immoral dynastic squabbles. Isolation from Europe's power games was reinforced in 1823 by the Monroe Doctrine, which declared that any European intervention in the Western Hemisphere would be regarded as an unfriendly act. This established the basis upon which the US eventually built what has often been described as hemispheric hegemony.

Isolationism, however, was a compromised policy. It was reserved for Europe. Elsewhere the US pursued ruthless expansion through hostilities with Indians, Canadians and Mexicans. War with Spain in 1898 brought the US control over the Philippines and Cuba and other islands in the Caribbean and the Pacific. There is little sign of isolationism here. Instead, policy was driven by a greed for both territory and economic gain and a desire to shine the beacon of liberty abroad.

By the end of the century, the US was a major naval power and both the spirit and practice of isolationism were under challenge. In 1899 and 1900, Secretary of State John Hay issued his famous 'Open Door' notes on China, demanding that the European powers should allow equal and open access there for American commerce. And, in 1904, President Theodore Roosevelt proclaimed his Corollary to the Monroe Doctrine, which asserted the right of the US to interfere in civil unrest in Western Hemisphere countries to restore order (and thus protect US economic interests). Such internationalism, articulated so publicly, placed isolationism under attack. In 1917, it received further blows when US faith in legalism and neutrality proved to be misplaced: German U-boat attacks on US shipping provided the immediate cause for US entry into the First World War (1914–18). However, the sympathies and interests of the Wilson administration had lain with the allies well before that and the President was also determined to participate in the peace treaties in order to remould the world according to his liberal principles.

In 1918, Wilson promulgated his famous Fourteen Points. They reconciled isolationism and internationalism by universalising US values. The Old World system was to be replaced by New World internationalism – free trade, self-determination of peoples, freedom of movement on commercial waterways and on the high seas, open diplomacy subject to democratic scrutiny and held accountable to the people, a just and charitable peace without reparations, and a collective security organisation – the League of Nations – to prevent war. Sadly for Wilson, wily Old World leaders compromised his vision and sceptical US politicians undermined collective security by refusing to ratify the Versailles Peace Treaty, thus preventing US participation in the League of Nations. Over the years, the US liberal and idealist democratic agenda has changed little from Wilson's vision, but how to prosecute it successfully has remained elusive. Tension between isolationism and internationalism still continues, though the Japanese attack on Pearl Harbor in December

1941, modern communications and the development of intercontinental ballistic missiles (ICBMs), the need for the global containment of communism, and the emergence of an interdependent world economy have pushed isolationism more and more to the fringes of influence.

Idealism and realism

As the US became powerful and involved in world affairs, more debate took place on how it should conduct its foreign policy. This was often couched in terms of realism versus idealism.

Realism is associated with Old World diplomacy. It draws on an analysis of human nature and a conception of the logic of geopolitical power relations. In a world where there is no Leviathan to impose order, each state must seek to maximise power to secure its own survival. Furthermore, states must both recognise that human beings have a tendency to conflict as they pursue their own interests and that weapons cannot be defined as intrinsically defensive or offensive: those who wield and face them decide that. Thus, in addition to the danger of predatory human behaviour, there is the problem that a state's defensive measures may be seen as potential for aggression by another, which then responds in kind and sets up the vicious circle of an arms race. This matrix of problems is the traditional geopolitical security dilemma.

As security of the state is the prime objective for the realist, and as the primary agent of protection in the anarchical international realm is the state, then the realist explains foreign policy in terms of the state's attempts to sustain itself by whatever means are available. Thus force, secret diplomacy, duplicity, balancing power or containing a superpower by allying with other states, and conduct contrary to democratic principles are all options to be explored in the prudent pursuit of national security. Other states must not be judged in terms of how friendly they are, or by their stated intentions, but by their power and the maxim that today's friend could become tomorrow's enemy and vice versa. Such a position is at odds with the oft-made claim that democracies do not war with each other.[4]

The realist approach has often been derided as amoral, but realists have two responses. First, in an imperfect world it is absurd to see moral agency as a choice between following or departing from moral principles. Instead, moral agency needs to be seen as a practical dilemma of choice between moral imperatives – to fight in a just cause, or 'thou shalt not kill'. Second, realists want to secure the state because they believe it is imbued with intrinsic moral worth: it creates order, which is the prerequisite for moral action. The crucial problem here arises when foreign policy means conflict with the moral ends of the domestic society to such an extent that they threaten its integrity.

Idealists have optimistic views of humanity and its potential for compromise, accommodation and rational action. US idealism stands for open diplomacy, human rights, economic development through the free market and the avoidance or containment of war, through international organisations, law and collective security. Underpinning all is a conviction that individuals are unique and precious and must not be treated as means to a politically defined end to which they do not subscribe: for example, at the horrendous extreme, the elimination of kulaks or Jews, for the 'greater good of society'. Idealism has been criticised for tending to elevate principles above careful calculation of national interests and achievable results (for example the Vietnam War[5]) and for failing to act prudently in an anarchical and dangerous international system. Seeing when it is necessary to depart from principles in order to defend the state and promote the general good in the longer term is the crucial issue here.

In more recent times, the realist–idealist debate has been developed further. First, neo-realists, who accept many of the basic assumptions of realism, focus more on the system, rather than human nature, and explain international relations in terms of the character and distribution of power in the anarchical state system (see Mearsheimer and Waltz in Chapter 10). Second, neo-liberals, who share many of the premises of traditional idealism, believe that there is the possibility of transcending the nation state security dilemma. They emphasise both the importance of building up trust, and the beneficial effects of complex economic interdependence, international regimes, law, and organisations.

Can the scope of US foreign policy be captured in a Manichaean-like division between isolationism and internationalism? Are there realists and idealists as characterised above? The answer to both questions is No! The fact that there is no clear dividing line between foreign and domestic policy necessarily impairs the isolationist-internationalist dichotomy. Similarly with idealism and realism, there is always a mixture of the two. No American realist has conducted foreign affairs without celebrating the rights, liberties and economic system of the US and allowing such values to influence policy. No idealist has sustained, in pristine form, their principles and moral values when confronted by the need to save the state they value. We thus need to be sensitive to the complexities involved here. Images of idealism and realism, isolationism and internationalism always need to be nuanced and should be used as analytical starting points rather than the end points of explanation.

While internationalism has been dominant since 1945, with only vestiges of isolationism in evidence, the struggle between idealism and realism in various forms has swung back and forth. So, there are no clear answers as to precisely which of these positions is at the heart of American foreign policy because they are in constant flux. However, while they may be travelling at different velocities, they are all still in circulation. They are all part of US foreign policy's intellectual lifeblood. Identifying that helps our understanding of both policy-makers and what is going on.

Who makes US foreign policy?

The Founding Fathers divided formal power in foreign policy between the Executive and the Legislature: the President and the State Department on the one hand and Congress on the other. The Judiciary has only a peripheral role. The Supreme Court has a watching brief, but it has never been assertive. The Curtis Wright Case in 1936 affirmed the President's use of broad powers, and in Nixon versus the United States (1973), the Court only claimed the right to decide what were appropriate grounds for a presidential claim of executive privilege to keep matters confidential: it did not question the privilege itself. Our main focus must therefore be on the executive branch led by the President and on the Congress. At the same time, we must remember that this is a dynamic system, which responds to external factors, technology, and domestic changes. Power to formulate foreign policy has thus shifted since 1945 within the bureaucracy, and back and forth between the legislative and executive branches. This has largely been caused by the different characteristics of incumbent presidents, foreign policy set-backs, such as the loss of China to communism and the Vietnam War, and, more recently, by the transition to a post-Cold War world. Also, a problem can determine the type of response required and that, in turn, determines who or what does the responding. This is well illustrated by the Cuban missile crisis (see Chapter 6).

The President is Commander-in-Chief (CIC) of the armed forces and chief diplomat, with the power to make nominations for diplomatic appointments and to negotiate treaties. He can also set policy through his State of the Union addresses and announcements such as the Truman Doctrine (1947). However, this list both overstates and understates presidential powers.

The distribution of power: the Congress

The President's power to commit US military forces overseas is extensive, but limited by both the Congress's constitutional prerogative to declare war and the War Powers Act (1973). The latter only allows a president to commit troops to action overseas for a maximum of ninety days without congressional approval. It was passed as a result of US involvement in Vietnam, where a *de facto*, but undeclared, war was fought (see Chapter 7). The Act's effectiveness, however, is questionable, not least because of practical difficulties involving the need to respond effectively and swiftly to events such as the Iranian hostage crisis (1980) and the Gulf War (1991). There are also legal complications. The Chadha Supreme Court Case (1983) declared congressional vetoes of Executive actions illegal. In short, it may be unconstitutional for the Congress to veto an order of the CIC that commits US troops to combat overseas.

It would be wrong, however, to suggest that the War Powers Act is without force, just as it would also be a mistake to overlook the potential effectiveness of constraints that pre-date it. Their potency depends on congressional willingness to assert and apply them vigorously. Bearing such points in mind, let us examine congressional powers in more detail.

i   Control of the purse strings: this is primarily exercised by the House of Representatives, but, except in extraordinary circumstances (in 1975 Congress refused President Ford's request for funds to help the crumbling South Vietnamese regime), it is an unwieldy device. Presidents can shift resources between areas of policy, or camouflage things through covert operations, and their lieutenants may even divert funds illegally (as in the Iran–Contra Affair 1985–86).

ii A Senate two-thirds majority vote is required to approve both presidential nominees for diplomatic appointments and treaties. Refusal to ratify treaties, as in the case of the Treaty of Versailles 1919, may be rare, but ratification may be so clearly impossible to get that the President abandons the effort (e.g. with the International Trade Organisation (ITO), 1950). Faced with such difficulties, presidents have resorted to executive agreements between heads of state (security pact with South Korea 1949). In 1954, the Bricker amendment tried to make executive agreements subject to the same kind of approval as treaties, but it fell one vote short in the Senate of the two-thirds majority needed for a constitutional amendment. By the 1970s the post-war average of executive agreements per year was over 2,000 compared with just over fifteen treaties, and the contents of many of the former were unknown outside of government. Disillusionment with the Executive because of Vietnam made it possible to pass the Case–Zablocki Act in 1972, which requires that the Congress be informed about all executive agreements. But this has not the conflict between State and the NSC for control over foreign policy has often been bitter. This was particularly so with Henry Kissinger as NSA in the first Nixon administration; during the open feud between Secretary of State Cyrus Vance (1977–80) and NSA Zbigniew Brzezinski (1977–81); and between White House staff and Secretary of State Alexander Haig (1981–82). At times the State Department has been relegated to conducting everyday affairs and helping to justify and defend policy made elsewhere in the bureaucracy. In the mid and late 1990s there were contradictory developments. Clinton's general preoccupation with domestic matters and attempts to return the NSC to a co-ordinating role tended to raise the profiles of Secretaries of State Warren Christopher and Madeleine Albright. Yet, at the same time, Congress championed financial cut-backs, staff reductions and some closures of diplomatic missions.

The NSC was set up to co-ordinate all aspects of national security and it has grown in stature over the years and drawn power away from the State and Defense Departments. However, presidents use the NSC differently and State can still be effective when run by someone like George Schultz, Secretary of State for much of the Reagan period. President Clinton's first NSA, Anthony Lake, tried to move the NSC back to a co-ordinating role, only to be criticised for failing to articulate clear policy priorities: his successor, Samuel (Sandy) Berger, has fared little better. Driven by an overly sensitive concern with public opinion, he has been accused of inconsistency and short-termism. With the post-war tendency towards highly personalised presidential power, the rise in importance of the NSA at the expense of unwieldy bureaucracies seems, in retrospect, to have been rather inevitable.

Other departments and agencies – the CIA, the Joint Chiefs of Staff and the Defense, Treasury and Commerce Departments – all have significant, but specialised inputs into foreign policy. In contrast, the President, the NSC, the NSA, and the State Department have broad remits, which is why they are so often decisive in policy formulation and execution. However, having identified the central core of the policy-making process, it is important to add that relationships within it fluctuate wildly. How it operates at any one time is determined by the President. Truman depended on the State Department and the NSC. Eisenhower used Dulles and the NSC, but was also unique in making significant use of the Cabinet. Kennedy relied on task forces, *ad hoc* committees and his NSA, McGeorge Bundy. For President Johnson the famous Tuesday luncheon meetings were vital policy-deciding events. For the following administration it was the Nixon–Kissinger axis that was at the heart of things. Ford gave more emphasis to economic constituencies in foreign policy-making, but also depended much on Secretary of State Kissinger.

Carter, rather unsuccessfully, tried to marry Secretary of State Vance's liberalism with NSA Brzezinski's hard realism. Reagan allowed a rather fractious NSC to compete with the State Department. Bush ran a much tighter ship, with James Baker and Lawrence Eagleburger as successive Secretaries of State. He pursued a pragmatic and rather conservative foreign policy, despite the New World Order rhetoric, through conventional channels. Under Clinton, the absence of Cold War certainties, which had done so much to determine priorities, has meant a more open political scenario with an enlarged intermestic agenda. Clinton clearly acknowledged this with the creation by executive order on 25 January 1993 of the National Economic Council (NEC), to co-ordinate policy-making processes with respect to domestic and international economic issues. Under Robert E. Rubin, the NEC soon proved itself to be a major force in foreign policy.

The changing context and the 'imperial' challenge to democracy

After the Second World War, the changing nature of foreign policy and its own expanded international role challenged the US. How it responded led some to conclude that constitutional restraints had snapped, that there was a growing rift between democratic principles and foreign policy practices, and that power had corrupted both the foreign and domestic domain.

The chief operational changes were in communications, technology, and nuclear weaponry, which concentrated power in fewer hands, centred on the President, rather than in the institutional establishment. Rapid communications and ICBMs also emphasised the need for swift and decisive responses to world crises such as the Berlin Blockade in 1948 and Soviet missiles in Cuba in 1962. This encouraged the creation of the NSC as a parallel bureaucracy more directly under the authority of the President and more responsive to his wishes and commands. Diplomats and foreign policy personnel were not redundant, but they were increasingly demoted to tasks involving routine affairs and technical matters and to collecting and disseminating information for high level talks conducted by their political bosses. Ask yourself: What are the dominant images of foreign policy in the post-war world? Almost without exception, what will come to mind are heads of state meetings such as the one between Clinton and Yeltsin in Moscow in 1995. This is the age of summitry, of diplomacy by presidents and prime ministers. Churchill, Roosevelt and Stalin invented it in wartime and it is radically different from diplomatic experience prior to 1939.

In this new operating environment, policy is conducted under the eye of the journalist and the TV camera. In a very real sense it has gone public. For democracies, this has raised the importance of public opinion in foreign policy-making and, thereby, produced two complications. First, expressions of approbation or opprobrium by the public or their elected representatives became more potent – something totalitarian opponents do not generally have to concern themselves with. Second, in sensitive diplomacy such as opening relations with the People's Republic of China (PRC) in 1972 (see Chapter 7) it became difficult to maintain secrecy, and that led to the use of less orthodox means. Ironically, the more intense public gaze has driven foreign policy into the less accountable and less visible channels of the NSC, the CIA and covert operations.

While enhanced communications and the White House rapid response bureaucracy helped to provide more flexibility, new substantive changes in foreign affairs, ideology, and nuclear weapons, had a contrary impact. Foreign policy relies upon overwhelming force or flexible negotiations to achieve its goals. In the post-war period, the US enjoyed neither of these luxuries in its dealings with the Soviet Union. American power was never sufficient to be able to dictate policy to the Soviets and both its ideology and nuclear deterrent created inflexibility.

The ideological rift between American and Soviet values left little room for manoeuvre. At the same time, the danger of nuclear war also meant that there was no leeway for mistakes. The US had to make its nuclear deterrent credible to the Soviets in clear and forthright terms. American leaders feared appeasement, which had brought the Pearl Harbor disaster and the Second World War to the US in the 1940s. Peace-loving democracies must not send the wrong message again. America thus had to be prepared, and be seen as willing, to fight for freedom. There would be implacable resolve to defend the rights and interests of the US against communism.

These conditions and convictions produced a bipolar world, which was reinforced by both an ideological and a nuclear stand-off. This model appealed to many US decision-makers because, among other reasons, it made it easier to mobilise and attract public support. It was also attractive to many scholars as complex events could be slotted into a neat explanatory paradigm with sharp analytical categories, but it fell far short of exhausting the complexities of the US–Soviet relationship, never mind what went on elsewhere.[6] The world was not that simple. Complicating factors proliferated as time went by. International organisations appeared, such as the UN, the International Monetary Fund (IMF), the North Atlantic Treaty Organisation (NATO), and the Conference on Security and Co-operation in Europe (CSCE), which emphasised the importance of multilateral diplomacy. Decolonisation created more states. New factors entered the international agenda such as over-population, under-development, disease, terrorism, sustainable growth and pollution. In addition to the ideological rift between East and West, other doctrines emerged: non-alignment, liberationism, and Islamic fundamentalism, as well as important differentiations within the Western and Eastern blocs. Finally, there was an awareness of the world's economic interdependence.

To deal with all of this, the US had a foreign policy capability that was checked and balanced by the Congress, law, and often by competing branches of the Executive. A two-centuries-old isolationist tradition had to be cast off and public opinion had to be mobilised in favour of a new global and very expensive foreign policy. In addition, policymakers had to work within the constraints of an inflexible ideology, fear of repeating the appeasement syndrome and the need to maintain the credibility of America's nuclear deterrent. Successive presidents got the job done, but the means created a new problem: the imperial presidency.

The response of the presidents

In their attempts to be effective, presidents have resorted to various techniques and styles of policy. Invoking national security has been used to justify much. It is a trump card empowered by loyalty to the nation. It should carry a warning: beware! Purging alleged communist sympathisers in the McCarthy witch-hunt, the illegal war in Cambodia (1970), and the Iran–Contra affair were all justified in the name of national security. It can be a means/end argument run amok.

Nurturing bipartisanship in Congress fostered similar dangers. Foreign policy was placed above adversarial politics and the pointed criticisms that accompany them. The result was swifter and more decisive foreign policy-making by the Executive and a generally (except for a renewal of partisan criticism during the Korean War) complacent and compliant Congress, at least until the Vietnam War. Bipartisanship is appropriate in times of acute crisis when the nation must pull together in order to survive – as in the Second World War – providing that even then it does not go too far. But long-term bipartisanship in peacetime draws the teeth of effective political control.

Presidents have also used the aura of office, the inherent powers of the CIC, the NSC, executive agreements, and dramatic announcements such as the Truman, Eisenhower, Carter and Reagan Doctrines, in order to effect policies. They have used covert operations and other secret channels to avoid the attention of the press and congressional oversight. And they have extracted area resolutions from Congress, which delegated vast discretionary powers to the President as CIC. These resolutions included Taiwan/Formosa (1955)[7], the Middle East (1957), and, most notoriously, the Gulf of Tonkin (1964), which enabled President Johnson to escalate the war in Vietnam.

Presidents thus developed a highly personalised style. The needs of national security in a world of dangers created by communism seemed to justify swift, effective, if at times extreme, measures, and an arrogant use of power. What seemed to have been forgotten was one of the foundational principles of the republic: good causes can only be achieved by good political means.

Arthur Schlesinger delivered a famous diagnosis of the malaise in *The Imperial Presidency*.[8] He claimed that the presidency had broken constitutional constraints: it was outside of the rule of law. Presidents had snatched war power from the Congress. By the time of Richard Nixon and the Watergate affair, the aphorism of absolute power corrupting absolutely was coming true. Corruption in foreign affairs spilt over into the domestic realm where Nixon attempted to justify his actions by invoking the national interest.

In the aftermath of Watergate, there was a resurgence of congressional assertiveness and a rekindling of the debate about how the US should conduct its foreign policy. The Congress tried to claw back some of its prerogatives through the Case–Zablocki Act and the War Powers Act, and by increasing its powers of congressional oversight. All helped to dethrone the imperial presidency, but for how long? During the Reagan period, policies in the hands of Colonel North ran out of control, as a small élite tried to divert funds illegally to sustain the anti-communist Contra rebels in Nicaragua. In the minds of North and his co-conspirators, their conception of national security overrode the mistaken democratic will of Congress.

This is a perennial problem for democracies. Abraham Lincoln struggled to reconcile interests of state with democratic values in the Civil War when he unconstitutionally suspended *habeas corpus*, arguing that violation of one law was justified if it meant that the constitution and the Union could be saved. In the end there is no easy solution to this problem. What really counts is judgement and the quality of the justification for departing from first principles in order to secure their long-term continuation. In the hands and in the judgement of an Abraham Lincoln we might feel that the values of democracy are more secure than in the hands and in the judgement of a Colonel North.

Conclusion

The question of who makes foreign policy cannot be answered without the intellectual context that was outlined in the opening sections of this chapter. That context tells us something about what to look for in terms of the style and some of the presuppositions and beliefs that decision-makers are likely to have: in a way it gives us an angle on who they are. However, even when structured into a coherent ideology, the relationship between beliefs and action is difficult to establish at a general level. Some scholars see ideology and action in a causal relationship. This is generally the case with New Left historians who place much emphasis on the dynamics of capitalism determining US policy (see Chapter 6). Others are less deterministic, seeing ideology as simply a tool for justifying actions *ex post facto*, or as one among a number of important variables in the explanation of US foreign policy behaviour. In contrast, realists believe that systemic structures of the international system explain foreign policy and that these variables override ideological beliefs (see Chapter 10).

In later sections of this chapter other signposts were erected, which indicate the likely places to look to discover which agency or department, or which office-holders, are formulating and conducting policy. The direction in which these signposts point will often be determined by both the character and disposition of whoever holds presidential office and the general contours of the international terrain, such as Cold War and post-Cold War worlds. Although the core, consisting of the President, the State Department, the NSC, the NSA, and now probably the NEC, will always be at the centre of things, other departments and agencies will be influential when matters pertaining to their expertise are at issue. In addition, often having impact on this institutional system are other influences, such as the media, public opinion, and lobbyists. Finally, weaving in and out of the interstices of policy-making runs the work of the Congress, consulting, advising, overseeing, empowering and restraining.

Although the traumas of the 1970s sensitised the Congress and the public to important problems to do with the evolution, formulation, and execution of foreign policy, and particularly to the problem of democratic control, they provided no easy or automatic answers. The Cold War superpower confrontation continued to provide national security grounds for an assertive and energetic foreign policy run by the Executive. With the end of the Cold War and the demise of the immediate security threat to the US, greater potential for constraining and democratically controlling the formulation and execution of policy seemed to emerge. The post-Cold War world challenged long-held convictions that the US must play a major international role, that the main priority of that role was and still is containment of potential challengers, and that national security demands a bipartisan consensus to empower the President to act vigorously and with a great deal of discretion in foreign policy. President Clinton, his NSA Anthony Lake, Secretary of State Warren Christopher, and Madeleine Albright, first as US Ambassador to the UN and then as Christopher's successor, all emphasised assertive UN multilateralism to deal with international problems and sponsored a policy of engagement and democratic and free-market enlargement to replace containment. But, these attempts to redefine US foreign policy only had limited success (see Chapters 9 and 10). The death of US troops in Somalia in 1993 led to disillusionment. There soon emerged a lack of consensus, a more partisan approach to foreign policy, and more concentration on economic issues, exports and jobs. This has drawn traditional domestic constituencies into the foreign policy arena, made direction of foreign policy more difficult, and injected democratic powers of control forcibly into the foreign policy-making field. For better or worse, what has been termed the constitutional invitation to struggle for power has been reintroduced into foreign affairs.

2   The US and the Cold War

Explanation and early containment, 1945–61

The Cold War was born in the mid-1940s: terminal illness took hold in 1989 and it expired in December 1991 along with the Soviet Union. But, what caused it? Was anyone or any state primarily to blame? Was it caused by historical enmity, economic rivalry, an ideological crusade, a geopolitical power struggle, or a complex mixture of all four?

Cold War: origins and containment

The historical fortunes of US–Soviet relations before 1945 were mixed, but on the whole antagonisms predominated. The US intervened, with other capitalist powers, on the side of the Whites in the Russian Civil War and refused to recognise the Soviet Union until 1933. After recognition relations improved, but then deteriorated badly because of Stalin's purges and show trials of the 1930s, the Nazi–Soviet pact of 1939 and the partitioning of parts of Europe that followed in its wake. From 1941–45 there was a Faustean pact against Nazi Germany. America acknowledged the huge Soviet cost of defeating the Germans and the Soviets were grateful for US Lend-Lease aid. Nevertheless, relations were still punctuated with disputes and suspicions. The Soviets feared that the British and Americans might make a separate peace with Hitler that would allow him to continue the war on the eastern front (a sort of Nazi–Soviet pact in reverse). When that did not happen they suspected that the West deliberately delayed D-Day to leave the Red Army to do most of the fighting against the *Wehrmacht*. For their part, the Americans were suspicious about the Katyn massacre, which slaughtered much of the Polish officer class (we now know that it was a Soviet and not a Nazi war crime), and about the pause of the Red Army before Warsaw, which allowed the Nazis to level the Ghetto and eliminate the pro-Western Polish Home Army. There were also recurrent mutual suspicions about post-war intentions.

Three clusters of economic facts were of great significance. First, the Soviet Union was devastated by war and hoped for economic assistance from the US. The Soviets were disappointed when the US abruptly stopped Lend-Lease aid after victory in Europe. This was required by American law, but the Soviets saw it as an unfriendly prelude to US demands for political concessions in return for aid: a tactic that President Truman did indeed pursue. Second, the US had become the world's economic colossus in the war. How to sustain that was of deep concern to US planners. They did not want a post-war recession resulting in the kind of social and political unrest that had fostered totalitarianism in the 1930s. The US wanted to internationalise New Deal reforms to make the face of capitalism acceptable and its performance more stable and accountable by exercising US management through the IMF and the General Agreement on Tariffs and Trade (GATT). Unfortunately, this economic vision was not compatible with that of the Soviets and, by 1946, they had rejected participation in the US grand capitalist design. Third, Europe needed economic reconstruction to promote self-help, otherwise the US would lose important markets and have to pour in endless resources to feed, house and clothe people. As Germany had the potential to be the economic powerhouse of Europe, logic dictated that its economy had to be revived. As most of it was in the West, its revival would unavoidably be perceived as a threat by the Soviets. However, the alternative for the US was an unacceptable dollar and humanitarian cost and a possible re-run of the inter-war tragedy if economic poverty and social unrest delivered Europe into the hands of political extremists.

The incompatibility of Western capitalism and Soviet communism, derived from different economic systems and clashing views on individual and collective rights, regained prominence once the overriding priority of defeating Germany and Japan had been achieved. Ideological differences surfaced not only over economic issues, but also over Poland and the treatment of the rest of Soviet-liberated Europe. Controversy arose about democracy and freedom. The West resented Soviet sway over Poland when Britain and France had, at least nominally, gone to war to safeguard it from Nazi totalitarianism. The Soviets, however, stipulated that the Polish government had to be 'friendly'. This was understandable given that the Soviet Union had been invaded three times in thirty years via Poland and had lost over twenty million people in the most recent attack. This security demand resulted in a Soviet-style democracy for Poland, which was hard for Americans to accept and contrary to what they thought had been agreed at the Yalta Conference in early 1945.

Geopolitical concerns were not the monopoly of Stalin; they had also troubled President Roosevelt for much of the war. He believed that it was imperative to co-opt the Soviets into post-war security arrangements. Those arrangements were an artful mixture of idealistic collective security apparatus and realist power politics. The UN looked like a collective security organisation where all would be responsible for each other's security, but effective policing depended upon great power unanimity. Derived from this realist view of power was the provision of the right of veto for the Soviet Union, the US, Britain, France and China – the permanent members of the Security Council. In addition, both Roosevelt and Truman expected that each great power would have primary responsibility, working with the UN, for its own area. In the US, internationalism might have triumphed over isolationism, but there was no US desire to remain in the heart of Europe.

The great problem with all this was how to maintain great power consensus. Immediately after the war, with France temporarily out of the power equation, China in the throes of civil war, and Britain weakened by her war effort, the key considerations were: Soviet power; US power; and the danger of a revival of German power. Once the Soviets and Americans began to fear each other's intentions, neither side could allow Germany to move fully within the other's camp. The potential power gain for one would have been unacceptable to the other. This was the reason that the German problem was such a sensitive issue and why partition became semi-permanent. But mutual suspicions and security fears spread wider than this. The Soviets did not have the atom bomb, but the Americans did, and that caused insecurity. They feared the economic prowess of the US and the danger of the spread of capitalism. And most of all they wanted security and they felt that the West was set to deprive them of that by interfering in Eastern Europe and by denying them any say in the occupation of Japan. Americans for their part had learnt the lesson that isolationism was not a viable policy. Consequently, they became deeply anxious as economic and political unrest spread through Western Europe and as Soviet rhetoric became stridently critical of the West. Their worries were compounded when the Soviets began to act unilaterally in Eastern Europe and made bids for strategic and economic gains in Turkey and Iran. Most of all, rather than an invasion by the Red Army, the Americans feared a Kremlin-inspired wave of internal commotion that would make Europe vulnerable to the spread of communism.

All these matters were made worse because the allied working relationship between Stalin, Roosevelt and Churchill was broken in 1945, first by the death of Roosevelt and then by the electoral defeat of Churchill. In April 1945, evidence of strained relations surfaced in a notorious meeting between President Truman and Vyacheslav Molotov, the Soviet Foreign

Minister, whom the President scolded for Soviet failure to keep agreements on Poland. However, for the first year or so after the war, it was the British, rather than the Americans, who took a strong line against the Soviets.[1] The US continued to try to reach an accommodation with the Soviets. Truman, despite the unpleasant scene with Molotov, sent Roosevelt's old trusted stalwart Harry Hopkins as a personal envoy to Moscow to try to sort out problems: the gesture was to little avail. Soviet dominance of Poland, confusion about the Potsdam Conference (1945) agreement about reparations, Soviet unilateral actions, their refusal to participate in the IMF, their demands on Turkey, and in early 1946 their refusal to abide by a wartime agreement to withdraw from northern Iran, all alarmed the US. With the UN rendered largely ineffective by the veto and an ideological divide, it became clear that the US would have to look after its own security affairs. After strong American demands, and suffering adverse publicity in the UN, the Soviets eventually withdrew from Iran, but Truman was now worried about their intentions. In Washington, hard-line anti-communists in the State Department were making their voices heard, especially after a belligerent call for Soviet rearmament by Stalin in February 1946. Prompted by Stalin's speech, George Kennan, a long-standing Soviet expert, wrote the most famous diplomatic message of modern times – the Long Telegram – from the US Moscow Embassy on 22 February. In it he warned of the Soviet Union's tendency to expansion and of the need for the US to oppose it resolutely. This articulated many of the inchoate fears and concerns in the minds of Washington officials. Winston Churchill then added to the anti-Soviet momentum in his famous speech at Fulton Missouri on 5 March 1946. Conjuring up apocalyptic dangers with his powerful rhetoric, he dramatically called for Anglo–American co-operation to resist Soviet communism and spoke of an iron curtain having descended from Stettin in the Baltic to Trieste in the Adriatic.

The US still did not commit itself unequivocally against the Soviets, but it acted with less regard for their sensitivities in prudent moves to safeguard Western interests. In December 1946, Bizonia was created by merging the British and American zones of occupation in Germany. On 24 February, Britain formally informed the US that it could no longer give military assistance to Greece and Turkey: two key countries where the Soviets were thought to have ambitions. In response to this, President Truman, in one of the most dramatic diplomatic announcements of all times, demonstrated internationalism's triumph over isolationism in the US by announcing a peacetime commitment to help Europe and to support Greece and Turkey. The Truman Doctrine pledged help to resist aggression from internal or external sources and more specifically provided assistance to replace Britain's.

In May 1947, William Clayton, Under-Secretary of State for Economic Affairs, reported that economic distress in Europe was widespread and far worse than anticipated. In his opinion, it would lead to political and social disaster unless action were taken. A month later, the new Secretary of State, General George Marshall, who was less conciliatory than his predecessor James Byrnes, proposed a European Recovery Programme in his famous Harvard Speech. This became the Marshall Plan. Technically, it was open to Soviet participation, but neither the US nor its closest ally, Britain, had any intentions of allowing them to take part. With the implementation of Marshall Aid came the economic division of Europe and, most important of all, of East from West Germany. This was highly provocative to the Soviets with the danger of capitalist infection spreading via a newly created *Deutschmark* into Eastern Europe. They reacted by closing ground access to the Western redoubt in Berlin, thus precipitating the first major Cold War crisis. The Western response was the Berlin airlift of June 1948 to May 1949. The Soviets also clamped down in the rest of Eastern Europe, removing, most notably in Prague, the last vestiges of pro-Western elements from government. In 1949, after much hesitation and pressure from their Western European allies, the US established NATO.

Ineluctably, lines were being drawn. A sequence of actions and reactions, security concerns and clashing ideologies, economic incompatibilities, difficult personalities, and the historical baggage of mutual suspicions were snatching defeat from the jaws of victory. War was to be succeeded by Cold War, not by peace. In July 1947, in *Foreign Affairs*, Kennan anonymously published an elaboration on his Long Telegram entitled 'The Sources of Soviet Conduct': 'Soviet pressure against the free institutions of the Western world is something that can be contained by the adroit and vigilant application of counter-force at a series of constantly shifting geographical and political points.'[2] This became known as containment and it developed into official policy, with the help of Kennan, as Director of the newly established State Department Policy Planning Staff (PPS). He believed that there were five key industrial centres in the world: the US; Britain; Germany and central Europe; Japan; and the Soviet Union. Four were in the West and one was in the East and this was the way things should remain. Elsewhere, the West could afford to be flexible, because points on the periphery were expendable.

Over the next forty-two years, containment policy went through various permutations along a continuum which stretched from selective flexible power responses to meet whatever threats were mounted by the enemy, to a commitment to massive retaliation against whatever breach of the containment line was made. Where the US should stand on this continuum preoccupied its strategists throughout the Cold War.

Truman and NSC-68

In 1950, the first important twist to US containment policy was effected, largely by Paul Nitze, Kennan's successor as Director of the State Department Policy Planning Staff. The inspiration for this major review was multifaceted. First, the international system had evolved into a rigid bipolar configuration that challenged Kennan's flexible version of containment. Second, the Truman administration needed a bold policy in order to overcome American isolationist sentiment and to deflect charges that it was 'soft' on communism, accusations which were emboldened by spy scandals and later by the onset of McCarthyism. Third, international events had deteriorated badly. While the Democrats had 'lost' China to Mao Zedong's communists in 1949, the Soviets had consolidated their power in Eastern Europe, challenged the West with the Berlin blockade and broken the American monopoly on the atomic bomb. Finally, a series of fears reflected a lack of confidence: fear of appeasement in the face of a new totalitarian challenge to democracy, fear that the economic crises of the 1930s might recur and lend weight to communism as a viable alternative to capitalism, and fear that decolonisation would weaken Britain and France and provide new opportunities for communism in the Third World.

The response to all these factors was National Security Council Resolution 68 (NSC-68), one of the most important, most debated and arguably the most seriously flawed documents in recent American history. Its general thrust was not new. Many of its objectives and assumptions had been set out previously in NSC-20/4 in November 1948: namely that the Soviets were intent upon expansionist strategies, the communist design meant that the Free World was in peril, and that it fell to the US to lead the resistance against the 'red menace'. The novelty of NSC-68 lay in its global reach, its military emphasis, and its harsh tone. This had three serious and dangerous implications for US containment policy. First, the flexibility of Kennan's original version was lost because, in transforming containment from a selective to a perimeter fence strategy, the traditional hierarchy of interests became so blurred that national and global security became indistinguishable. Thereafter, policymakers persistently failed to distinguish between geopolitical and ideological containment. Second, militarisation had profound implications for the means by which the US would combat communism. To rely on nuclear weapons threatened to lead the US into an appeasement trap because, unless it were prepared to start nuclear war as an indiscriminate response to every challenge, irrespective of the importance of the interests at stake, it would be forced to yield to Soviet pressure. Each time that happened, it would lose credibility and invite the Kremlin to push harder, particularly as the Soviet nuclear arsenal began to offset the strategic advantage of the American. Consequently, contrary to Kennan's ideas, the US and its allies had to develop conventional force capabilities to supplement the nuclear deterrent and be prepared and able to act wherever communism threatened. This militarised version of containment dominated both the rest of the Cold War and American society as a vast military-industrial complex developed to service the demands of NSC-68. Third, the 'tone' of NSC-68 was couched in apocalyptic terms: 'The issues that face us are momentous, involving the fulfilment or destruction not only of the Republic but of civilisation itself.'[3] *Per force* America needed to take the initiative against communism and to change the nature of the Soviet system through a range of activities, including psychological and economic warfare, political pressure, and covert operations. Moreover, NSC-68 formulated a Cold War calculus based on a 'zero-sum game', whereby any gain for communism would be a loss to the West. It was thus important that any negotiations with the Soviets should be from a position of overwhelming strength so as not to lose any ground, either literally or psychologically. The image and credibility of the US were more significant than ever before because policy-makers were convinced that perceptions of change in the balance of power were just as damaging as quantifiable ones. In other words, the US had constantly to send the right signals and warnings to allies and enemies alike in order to give the appearance and/or reality of either maintaining the *status quo* or improving the West's position.

Had it not been for the outbreak of the Korean War in June 1950, it is extremely unlikely that NSC-68 would have secured the backing of Congress because of the vast expense involved (see Chapter 7). Once approved, though, its effects were profound and obvious. In the short-term, defence expenditure mushroomed to over $50 billion, or 18.5% of US GNP. To maintain the American strategic supremacy, Truman approved the development of the hydrogen bomb and US commitments overseas were increased, most notably by the decision to fight a land war in Asia to repel communism from South Korea (see Chapter 7). Also, to enhance the capabilities of the Free World, new alliances were sought and existing ones strengthened. In September 1950, America bolstered its commitment to conventional defence in Europe, in part to give heart to allies there and in part to persuade them to accept West German remilitarisation. Furthermore, to counter criticism of the loss of China, the Truman administration took a hard, even provocative, line against Mao. In June 1950, the US Seventh Fleet was ordered to patrol the Taiwan Strait. This reversed Truman's gradual disengagement during the late 1940s and re-committed American support to Chiang Kai-shek's nationalists, who Mao had driven from the Chinese mainland onto Taiwan.

In the longer term, NSC-68 both secured a bipartisan consensus in foreign policy which would endure for two decades, except for a brief partisan skirmish over General MacArthur's conduct of the Korean War, and set the contours of American strategy for the remainder of the Cold War. It also successively secured the primacy of security above all other aspects of the budget, the militarisation of containment, and America's coming of age as a global policeman. However, the internal inconsistencies and oversimplifications in NSC-68 meant that it also bequeathed a series of problems to subsequent administrations. Significantly, Kennan did not endorse NSC-68.

NSC-68's vision of a monolithic, Kremlin-dominated, world communism caused the US to misinterpret international affairs and to neglect opportunities to exploit fragmentation within the communist camp. The blurring of national with global security interests meant that instead of enhancing US security through an arms build-up, NSC-68 disproportionately increased US commitments and provided a dangerous recipe for over-extension. The prescription that the US should only negotiate from a position of overwhelming strength provoked legitimate Soviet security fears and ran counter to the hopes of some Americans of socialising them into the existing international system. Furthermore, NSC-68 exposed the US to charges of hypocrisy and perversion of its own values. The authors of NSC-68 claimed that the US was disadvantaged significantly *vis-à-vis* the Soviet Union because the Kremlin had no moral standards other than those which served the communist revolution. Yet, at the same time, they declared that 'The integrity of our system will not be jeopardised by any measures, covert or overt, violent or non-violent, which serve the purpose of frustrating the Kremlin design … '.[4] Most dangerously of all, NSC-68 failed to distinguish between geopolitical and ideological threats and thus, in the brutal frankness of J.L. Gaddis, made 'all interests vital, all means affordable, all methods justifiable.'[5] Just how a constitutional democracy could subscribe to this and still hold true both to itself and its self-proclaimed moral superiority was a question that troubled successive administrations throughout the Cold War.

Eisenhower and the New Look

Eisenhower largely endorsed NSC-68. He accepted its monolithic view of international communism and the dangers it identified of communist subversion. He became extremely fond of the imagery of nations toppling successively to communism like a row of up-ended dominoes. Eisenhower also believed that a communist victory anywhere was a triple defeat for the West: a potential ally was lost, an implacable enemy gained a new recruit, and US credibility was damaged. Furthermore, his Secretary of State, John Foster Dulles, epitomised a missionary vision whereby the world aspired to be like America and America had to champion the rights of both the voiceless and, at times, unenlightened. In fact, the battle between 'right' and 'wrong' was so clear that Dulles had little time for either non-alignment or neutrality, concepts he regarded as short-sighted and immoral.

However, Eisenhower's New Look strategy, which emerged in 1953 from a government review called Operation Solarium, did differ significantly from its predecessor in several respects. It rejected the profligacy of NSC-68 with its assumption that 20% of GNP could be devoted to defence. The Republicans were committed to balanced budgets and tax cuts and Eisenhower was personally convinced that the US people would not sanction an indefinite sacrifice for an unwinnable war, which is what defensive containment seemed to entail. Whereas Truman had justified massive expenditure on the grounds that it was the threat of communism, rather than bankruptcy, which challenged America, Eisenhower warned that care had to be taken that waging containment did not impose so many demands upon the American economy that it destroyed the very system that it was trying to defend. This was all too possible if the budget got out of hand, or if rigid regimentation were necessary to harness productive capacity, or if the US got sucked into unwinnable and costly wars. Indeed, Eisenhower's first major contribution to this approach was to end the expensive and futile fighting in Korea. Thereafter, he cut back on military personnel and reined in military expenditure so successfully that throughout his administrations the defence budget remained significantly lower than Truman's, ranging between $35–42 billion.

The crux of the New Look was thus to accept the principles of NSC-68 but to prosecute them in ways that did not overburden American society. The result was that Eisenhower's containment strategy had three key themes: renewed focus on nuclear weapons, burden-sharing with allies, and covert, economic and psychological warfare. Eisenhower took the US back to a reliance on its superiority in air power and nuclear weapons, so much so that he and Dulles conceived of small nuclear bombs as tactical weapons to be deployed in the event of a European conflict. The deterrent of massive atomic and thermonuclear retaliation had the double advantage of being cheaper than conventional forces and reducing reliance on overseas bases. Eisenhower authorised the B41, equivalent to 400 Hiroshima-type bombs, doubled the size of the US nuclear stockpile between 1953 and 1955, and deployed low-kiloton nuclear warheads in Europe that could be used as tactical weapons in a limited war. Dulles, in an aphorism for which he became infamous, proclaimed that the art of Cold War statecraft had become brinkmanship: 'The ability to get to the verge without getting into war is the necessary art.'[6]

The corollary to massive retaliation was to devise ways to retain some semblance of flexibility at minimum cost, particularly in the battle for the Third World. This came in three forms. First, the US looked increasingly to alliances and regional co-operation. It was important to share the burden of global containment, particularly in the Middle East where the US struggled to project unilateral power. It was important, too, to develop and display a sense of shared purpose in order to encourage resistance to communist subversion, to deter Soviet encroachment, and to subdue regional internecine disputes for the sake of a common front against communism. The ultimate aim was to encircle the Soviet Union and China with states aligned with the US. This would erect a perimeter fence and allow other states to man it with their, rather than US, conventional forces. With this objective in mind, the US secured the integration of West German forces into NATO to bolster the European theatre. In the Middle East, it sponsored the Northern Tier and the Baghdad Pact (later CENTO). For Asia, it promoted both the South East Asia Treaty Organisation (SEATO), comprised of Britain, Australia, New Zealand, Pakistan, France, the Philippines and Thailand, and continued the ANZUS Pact concluded by Truman with New Zealand and Australia. These arrangements were supplemented further by several bilateral defence arrangements with countries such as Japan, South Korea and Nationalist China.

The second way to retain flexibility was to seize the Cold War initiative. The Republicans had criticised containment as 'negative, futile and immoral' because it did nothing for those enslaved by communism. In contrast, Dulles laced his public declarations with aggressive rhetoric about 'liberation' and 'rolling-back' the frontiers of communism. This was predominately psychological warfare with the triple hope that, by striking various poses and sending messages, it would be possible to galvanise the American public, reassure American allies and discomfort the Soviet regime. However, Dulles' aspirations were also underpinned by what became a hallmark of Eisenhower's presidency: covert operations. The CIA helped to overthrow governments in Iran in 1953 and

Guatemala in 1954 and tried, but without success, to do the same in Indonesia in 1958. It was also involved in guerrilla activities in North Vietnam, promoted disorder in Eastern Europe and monitored sections of both American and allied societies.

The final means to avoid dangerous rigidity was an effort to reduce tensions with the Soviets and to regulate the conduct of the Cold War. This strategy derived from Eisenhower's concerns about an unsustainable arms race and apparently auspicious changes in the international system, notably the winding down of the war in Korea, Stalin's death, and allied arrangements which allowed West Germany to enter NATO and rearm. During his presidency, Eisenhower held three summits with Soviet leaders, there were five foreign ministers' meetings, and a series of lower level talks ranging from arms control to culture. Cynics have interpreted Eisenhower's willingness to parley with the Soviets, in his later years in office, as just another form of psychological warfare. For example, they claim that his Open Skies initiative at the first Cold War summit in Geneva in July 1955, which proposed aerial surveillance of military installations to minimise the threat of a surprise attack, was an attempt to embarrass the Soviets, who were unlikely to accept. Others have seen in Eisenhower's policy efforts towards a limited form of *détente*. But, his commitment to *détente* was questioned by the cavalier use of U-2 reconnaissance planes over the Soviet Union in the run-up to the Paris Four Power Summit in May 1960. When a plane was brought down by the Soviets on 1 May, only two weeks before the summit, it created such a diplomatic furore that the conference was aborted. Despite that fiasco, it is clear that Eisenhower at least abandoned Truman's insistence on negotiating only from a position of overwhelming strength.

All things considered, the New Look attempted 'containment on the cheap'. Truman's policy had been an assured response calculated to meet, but not exceed, the initial provocation wherever it might take place. Eisenhower's policy maintained certainty of response, but introduced uncertainty as to place and nature. The gamble was that uncertainty would breed Soviet caution and gain the US the initiative. Eisenhower was relatively successful. The defence budget was controlled, the US did not become embroiled in another foreign war, and relations with the Soviets were relatively peaceful – despite the US brandishing nuclear weapons over Korea and Taiwan, and the Soviets over the Suez Crisis in 1956.

Conclusion

It may well be that good luck as much as good judgement was on Eisenhower's side because he failed to address many of the contradictions bequeathed him by NSC-68. The Republicans contracted US means to prosecute containment short of nuclear retaliation, but actually increased US commitments through their alliance policy. Their rhetoric about 'roll-back' alarmed allies and raised false hopes, sometimes with disastrous effects, such as in the 1956 Hungarian uprising. Blind acceptance, at least in public, of monolithic communism, prevented a more enlightened China policy and jeopardised US integrity in the Third World. Here a combination of the moral crusade necessary to mobilise the American public and the inability of policy-makers to distinguish between nationalist and communist liberation movements, swept the US into a posture pitted against both change and its traditional anti-colonial values. Furthermore, brinkmanship, relying predominantly on nuclear weapons, was dangerously rigid, held potentially disastrous consequences, and was morally repugnant for many. Indeed, it forced consideration of a first strike strategy and the treatment of nuclear weapons as conventional weapons, despite the fact that NATO war games revealed that even a limited nuclear conflict would destroy most of central Europe.

By the 1960s, emphases in US Cold War policy were changing in response to developments in the communist world. On 4 October 1957, the Soviets had launched Sputnik 1, thus demonstrating their technical ability to develop ICBMs. The Soviets were rapidly closing the technological gap with the Americans and gradually creating a nuclear stalemate. At the same time, both the Soviets and the Chinese were busy supporting Third World liberation movements. The Cold War confrontation now focused on the problem of dealing with nuclear power that could inflict unacceptable damage on each side if war were to come, and with winning the hearts and minds of the Third World. These were the challenges that were to confront John Kennedy and his successors.

3 Superpower collaboration and confrontation

US containment policy, 1961–91

The Kennedy administration oversaw a qualitative change in the nature of the Cold War and a turning point in containment policy. The development of Mutual Assured Destruction (MAD) shifted the emphasis from outright victory to that of managing an enduring balance between East and West. The new 'logic' of the Cold War was for a peaceful resolution and this, for US policy-makers, signalled the end of the drive for victory through military preponderance. MAD compromised the threat of massive retaliatory power and, as the Cuban missile crisis demonstrated in 1962, generated unacceptable levels of brinkmanship. Instead, the onus fell upon collaboration with the Kremlin to assure system stability. Core US–Soviet relations had to be kept in mutually accepted balance at the same time that their intense competition was fought out on the Cold War periphery, such as in Vietnam.

Although it was never explicitly explained to the American people, containment policy became less about winning, and more about not losing the Cold War. Successive administrations accepted the need for system stability and perpetuated an East–West stand-off. They differed, though, over what mechanisms would best produce and maintain this. Where and how should the US fight in the periphery? How could destabilisation in the periphery be prevented from spilling back to the core relationship? How could public support be maintained for a seemingly unwinnable war against communism, especially once Vietnam tore American society apart? These types of calculation spawned the variety of strategies in later containment policy – flexible response, *détente*, the 'Second Cold War', and 'status quo plus'. And the assumptions that underpinned these strategies help explain why the end of the Cold War came so unexpectedly.

Kennedy, Johnson and flexible response

Kennedy's approach to the Cold War, encompassed by the slogan the 'New Frontier', focused on two things: MAD and the battle for the hearts, minds and capabilities of the Third World. In both of these aspects Kennedy wanted the capacity for flexible response, and it was clear in the run-up to the 1960 presidential election that his differences with Eisenhower were rooted in means not ends. Kennedy subscribed willingly to containment strategy, the domino theory, and the zero-sum calculus. He recognised the importance of alliances and tended towards a monolithic view of communism, regardless of increasingly obvious Sino-Soviet tension. He also accepted, particularly after the 1962 Cuban missile crisis, the need both to negotiate ground rules with the Soviets for the conduct of the Cold War and to stabilise nuclear relations, something epitomised by the Limited Nuclear Test Ban Treaty of 1963. What Kennedy took issue with was Republican unwillingness to fund the resources necessary to maintain American strategic supremacy and to win the battle for the Third World. He accused Eisenhower successively of allowing a missile gap to develop with the Soviet Union, of adopting a passive or reactive containment policy, and of so starving conventional American forces that the US was helpless in the face of 'brushfire challenges'. So great had the gap between means, perceived interests and commitments become, that Kennedy was convinced that US credibility was in the balance.

Kennedy and his highly influential Defence Secretary, Robert McNamara, felt that Eisenhower had taken the US back to the 1940s with a choice between humiliation and nuclear war. Their approach, rather like Truman's, was to develop the means for flexible response. Eisenhower's balanced budgets and low inflation were meaningless when the communist threat remained undiminished and American workers were repeatedly laid off through no less than three economic recessions. Instead, Keynsian economic policies could fulfil Kennedy's commitment to full employment and economic expansion whilst also empowering the hands of US policy-makers to protect America's global interests. Fortuitously, the Berlin and Cuban crises justified Kennedy's spiralling defence expenditure in the same way that the Korean War had Truman's.

Foremost among Kennedy's concerns was the missile gap, which later proved to be fictional. It was based on exaggerated beliefs in the prowess of Soviet technology fostered by the launch of sputnik into earth orbit and by the US Gaither Report in 1957. Before the fiction became clear, though, Kennedy moved quickly to counter this perceived 'window of vulnerability'. He approved an accelerated strategic missile build-up sufficient to guarantee the US an indisputable second-strike capacity: the US would be able to absorb a Soviet first strike and still be able to mount a devastating response. The theory was that nuclear relations with the Soviets could be stabilised by MAD, whereby deterrence was based on mutual vulnerability rather than the US supremacy of the Truman years. In 1961, the defence budget increased by 15% and, by 1964, the Polaris submarine fleet and the number of Minuteman missiles had almost doubled. Also, in 1964, McNamara revealed plans for a long-range missile force of over 1700 delivery vehicles – 1000 Minuteman I and II ICBMs, 54 land-based Titan IIs and 656 Polaris Submarine- Launched Ballistic Missiles (SLBMs).

Coupled with the nuclear build-up was a major commitment to fighting communism in the Third World, where the battle was characterised by subversion, guerrilla warfare, and clientelism. Whereas Dulles had simply opposed communism when it arose, Kennedy's idealism committed him to treating the cause as well as the effects. For dealing with the effects, he increasingly emphasised non-military and non-conventional elements of containment, particularly the expansion of counter-insurgency techniques that were epitomised by the Green Berets and Jungle Warfare Schools in the Panama Canal Zone and at Fort Bragg. For treating the cause, Kennedy prescribed economic aid and educational activities. These included the Peace Corps, which by 1963 had dispatched 9000 volunteers to over forty countries, and the Food for Peace project which used American agricultural surpluses to aid the Third World, albeit netting the US $1.5 billion annually in return. Most ambitiously of all, Kennedy wanted to nation-build around progressive movements so that the US could champion rightful claims to independence rather than support the conservative regimes used predominantly by Eisenhower. For this programme Kennedy drew intellectually on the work of Walt Rostow and his book *Stages of Economic Growth*[1] and signalled out Latin America for special attention. There he launched his most enterprising project: the Alliance for Progress (see Chapter 6).

Flexible response became the hallmark of the Kennedy and Johnson administrations but, for all the former's idealism and the latter's political savvy, their brand of containment was no less flawed than their predecessors'. Some mistakes were inherited. For example, they both had oversimplistic views of communism and of the international system and failed to distinguish between geopolitical and ideological threats. This had tragic implications for Johnson in Vietnam and caused Kennedy major problems in Latin America where his liberal idealism ran into America's vested interest in the *status quo*. Diversity could be tolerated only if it were either controlled by America or followed economic and political principles broadly in line with the American model.

Kennedy and Johnson's version of containment also brought new problems. Insistence on an indisputable 'second strike' capacity marked a major lurch toward MAD and necessitated massive expenditure. Also, the failure to establish a hierarchy of interests had enormous consequences. First, it caused Kennedy and Johnson to mortgage US credibility with ever increasing instalments to buy victory in Vietnam. Second, it put intolerable strains on the economy and American people, which Eisenhower had warned against doing. In the 1960s, the US could bear the costs of Kennedy's flexible response even less than it could the cost of Truman's NSC-68 in 1950. The US balance of payments problem deteriorated because of swollen military budgets and confidence declined in both the dollar and American leadership. Allies became harder to control and domestic opposition to the Vietnam carnage jeopardised bipartisan support for containment. Indeed, Johnson's decision not to seek re-election in 1968, and the plethora of anti-war incidents, signalled to many that containment was in crisis.[2]

Nixon, Ford, Carter and *détente*

The Nixon, Ford and Carter years marked the second major and long overdue shift in containment strategy. Whereas the Eisenhower, Kennedy and Johnson administrations were all variations on a theme set out in NSC-68, under Nixon new interpretations as well as tactics emerged. The most important of these was an effort to address the problem caused by NSC-68's failure to distinguish between geopolitical and ideological threats. This timely overhaul of defective US assumptions was due to a symbiotic relationship between world and domestic events. Abroad, the American position was in jeopardy. The Soviets were about to achieve nuclear parity. Vietnam was unwinnable and Nixon had the thankless task of securing 'peace with honour'. Furthermore, American weakness and a seemingly less aggressive Soviet posture tempted the alliance system to unravel. On the one hand, militarily weak organisations such as SEATO and CENTO were a constant drain on America's depleted resources. On the other, economic boom in Western Europe and Japan and their serious opposition to American policy in Vietnam and the Middle East meant an increasing challenge to US leadership. As for the home front, the backlash against the Vietnam experience ushered in a new era of popular neo-isolationism. The American people would not tolerate the overseas commitments necessary to maintain a global perimeter fence. Moreover, Congress moved to reassert its control over the presidency through measures such as the War Powers Act and renewed vigour in its role of executive oversight.

In short, relative economic decline and the end of the bipartisan foreign policy consensus meant that, when waging containment, Nixon, Ford and Carter operated under far greater constraints than any of their predecessors. This prompted a long overdue review of national interests, monolithic communism, and the nature of the international system. The Nixon Doctrine, promulgated in July 1969, tried to reduce the damaging expectation-capability gap created by American over-extension. The US would provide the nuclear deterrent for the West and honour its treaty commitments in the event of non-nuclear confrontation, but it would not necessarily provide manpower to stave-off communist aggression. Nixon's declaration also demonstrated a marked shift away from the zero sum calculations of previous administrations. In an era of reduced US capability and confidence, Kennan's ideas were resurrected: it was no longer accepted that every battle had to be won, or even fought, to maintain the East–West balance.

New assessments of both power and the international system closely accompanied this attempt to rediscover the hierarchy of US interests so carelessly sacrificed by NSC-68. In 1972, Nixon recognised that bipolarity was breaking down. He also deduced rightly from American impotence in Vietnam, from MAD's effect on the use of nuclear weapons, and from the shockwaves of the energy crisis in 1973, that a multidimensional calculation of power was necessary. Moreover, communist China was now too powerful to be ignored and should be engaged with in order to help balance Soviet power. Together, recognition of these realities offered new hope of containing communism without bankrupting the US. In many ways, the US had gone full circle and returned to Kennan's original hypothesis: five centres of power – now the US, Western Europe, Japan, China, and the Soviet Union – balancing each other and with flexibility around the periphery. This provided more opportunity for trade-offs to mitigate tension and an opportunity to shape a New World Order that would recognise the legitimate security concerns of all states, including the Soviet Union.

Perhaps the most radical rethink concerned the role of ideology in defining threats and interests: Nixon and Ford 'down-graded' it. Carter tried to redefine its role. At one stage, he was concerned less with notions of East–West conflict than with human rights and idealistic notions of a global community based upon economic welfare co-operation in an interdependent world. It has been claimed that the Nixon–Ford move away from justifying US foreign policy in terms of an ideological crusade marked the 'socialization of American foreign policy by the state system.'[3] In fact, it was a pragmatic adjustment to a peculiar combination of faltering American power, international systemic change, and a period of neo-isolationism in which anti-communism was no longer a galvanising 'clarion call'. The most important outcome of this was that the US re-established a hierarchy of interests based on calculations of geopolitical power rather than the confusion of NSC-68.

The resulting policy, known as *détente*, was defined by NSA Henry Kissinger as the evolution of 'habits of mutual restraint, coexistence, and, ultimately, co-operation.'[4] Again, the ultimate goal was containment, but this time it was conducted in a long series of US–Soviet summits. A combination of American resolve and inducements aimed to integrate the USSR into the very international system that US policymakers had long been convinced the Soviets were determined to overthrow. The most prominent characteristic of US policy was Kissinger's use of linkage, a negotiating strategy rooted in the American reversion to a more flexible containment strategy. Relieved of zero sum calculations, Kissinger was able to engage the Soviets in a series of talks, each conditional on the other, so that trade-offs could be secured and increased co-operation established through a complex 'carrot and stick' style diplomacy.

In terms of inducements, *détente* was designed to supplant bipolar conflict with new agreements and rules that enhanced each country's stake in co-operation with the other. For example, food and technology were to be used as non-military weapons to socialise the Soviet Union into the existing order, perhaps in the long-term even to make it partially reliant on Western markets. Even more prominent, though, were direct negotiations to reduce East–West tension, particularly in the field of nuclear weapons. The Soviets were approaching parity and the US feared the cost of a renewed arms race. Nixon and Kissinger thus accepted sufficiency rather than supremacy and negotiated with the Soviets to sustain MAD – hence moves to control nuclear proliferation and limit anti-ballistic missile systems (ABMs). Indeed, the symbol of *détente* became Strategic Arms Limitation, and in May 1972 Nixon and Brezhnev duly signed SALT I, which consisted of sixteen articles designed to limit ABMs and establish interim agreements to limit offensive strategic missiles.

The counterpart to the 'carrot' was the 'stick' – American resolve – and this was demonstrated in several ways. First, there was a great show of fulfilling commitments, such as aiding Israel in the 1973 Yom Kippur War and escalating the Vietnam conflict in order to negotiate for peace from a position of strength. Second, and much more audacious, were Kissinger's policy of linkage and attempts to play communist states off against one another. The most dramatic move in this strategy was the opening of relations with Communist China. Trade-offs and co-operation with the Soviets were underwritten by using the threat of a Sino-American alliance to apply pressure on Moscow to abide by the rules. This threat was made particularly plausible as China squared up with the Soviet Union on the Manchurian border and laid claims to the leadership of world communism. Nixon's trip to Peking in 1972 marked a revolution in containment strategy and ended one of the most absurd charades of post-war US foreign policy: that Taiwan was China and that the world's most populated country did not officially exist.[5]

Overdue enlightenment was thrust upon the Nixon, Ford and Carter administrations by international and domestic circumstances, but *détente* nevertheless marked a logical adjustment of containment strategy. Ends and means were better aligned. The escape from ideology dispelled the handicapping misperception of monolithic international communism. Focus on the Kremlin as the only power capable of destabilising the international order, as conceived of by Nixon and Kissinger, enabled a rationalisation of US commitments and alliance obligations. And by combining 'carrot and stick' measures, a credible attempt was made to fulfil the containment aim of socialising the Soviets into the international system.

The major problem of *détente* was thus not so much internal inconsistency, as in NSC-68, but the unwillingness of key actors to accept it. Within America, a whole series of conservative and vested interests lined up against *détente*. These included the conservative right, the powerful Zionist lobby, the US military, and the still-influential Cold War warriors, epitomised by Paul Nitze's Committee on the Present Danger, which in 1979 campaigned against Carter's defence and arms control policies. Abroad, it was still unclear to what extent Moscow controlled communist-leaning liberation movements, an uncertainty which helped persuade Nixon to continue the Vietnam war for four years and to unleash the CIA to destabilise the freely-elected Chilean government of Salvador Allende. More importantly, there was uncertainty about whether the Soviets would, or could, implement *détente* fully.[6] Suffering severe economic problems, they had a vested interest in co-operation but, at the same time, *détente* weakened common threat perceptions and, consequently, increased the difficulties of holding the Eastern bloc together.

Détente's denouement began with its association with Nixon and the Watergate scandal and ended with Carter's failed attempt to use it to pursue a more moral and principled foreign policy agenda. In part this was due to contradictions within Carter's foreign policy which saw him torn between pushing human rights, reaching diplomatic settlements with the Soviets, and guaranteeing sufficient military power to protect national security. For example, Carter welcomed Soviet dissidents and former political prisoners to the White House until Moscow retaliated by cooling US–USSR relations and cracking down harder on internal dissent.[7] However, there were other obstacles too. Congress sabotaged the hopes of Presidents Ford and Carter of using economic incentives to socialise the Soviet Union when the Senate insisted on the Jackson–

Vanik amendment, which made a trade agreement conditional upon the Soviet Union allowing more Jewish emigration. This was totally unacceptable to the Soviets because it was tantamount to interference in their internal affairs. Also, the American right led an assault on Carter's idealism and his allegedly weak handling of defence and foreign affairs. For example, they castigated his conduct of the Iranian hostage disaster, which began in 1979 in the wake of the Islamic fundamentalist revolution against the Shah's Iran, a US client state. Likewise, critics of *détente* seized upon the so-called Soviet offensive in the Third World as evidence of Kremlin duplicity and the dangerous naïveté of Carter's attempt to move the entire basis of foreign policy from 'power to principle'. From the mid-1970s onwards, the US suffered set-back after set-back on the periphery, from the fall of Saigon in 1975 to a series of communist advances in Africa and the Sandinista revolution in Nicaragua. By the time the Soviets sent 85,000 troops into Afghanistan, Carter's concern for human rights had become his Achilles' heel and the President was in full retreat from *détente* and swinging violently to a new hard-line. High technology sales were halted, feed grain shipments were embargoed and America boycotted the 1980 Moscow Olympics. While this failed to save either Carter or the SALT II treaty, which was pending ratification in the Senate, it laid the platform for Ronald Reagan's 'Second Cold War'.

Reagan and the Second Cold War

When Reagan came to office the Second Cold War was already underway. Accusations that the 1970s, the 'decade of neglect', had left America defenceless were false: Carter had reversed the post-Vietnam slump in the defence budget and in 1980 expanded it to $127 billion. Nevertheless, Reagan tapped successfully into US needs to be purged of Vietnam, to see an end to 'weak' post-Watergate leadership, and to shake off the paralysing self-doubt imbued by an America in decline. The Reagan Doctrine and the revolutionary Strategic Defence Initiative (SDI) captured the imagination of a disillusioned American public. Reagan promised 'dynamic self-renewal' and his prescription was simple: recovery of military supremacy, renewal of messianic purpose, and a return to free enterprise. Containment was central in all of these things. Rearmament needed a purpose to convince Congress to fund it. Scaremongering about the Soviet threat did just that. The need to contain a rejuvenated threat to American values promised to recover the sense of common purpose and pride in the American way of life that had pervaded the early Cold War years. Finally, containment provided justification for using free markets rather than aid to foster development in the Third World; as Reagan liked to argue, governments did not solve problems, they subsidised them.

However, while Reagan's strategy for containment is clear, his tactics are not. Analysis is handicapped by lack of primary sources and plagued by the 'Reagan paradox': the contradictions between his warmongering rhetoric and practical 'peace-making', his New Right creed and operational pragmatism,[8] and his invocation of the 'evil empire' and a generally well-managed, if not always friendly, relationship between the superpowers during his administrations. In addition, Reagan was one of the most ineffective presidents of all time when it came to dealing with disputes within his administration: 'No Reaganite "grand plan" shines through this fog' of policy muddle, bureaucratic disorder and his spectacular but disingenuous gestures.[9] For containment this meant contradictory policies as hard-liners such as Defence Secretary Caspar Weinberger pushed remorselessly for aggressive confrontation whilst influential moderates, such as Secretary of State George Schultz and ultimately Reagan, pushed for selective containment and a resurrection of linkage.

Nonetheless, broad themes can be discerned. Reagan re-emphasised ideology and placed moral crusade at the forefront of containment policy. At his first White House press conference, he accused the Soviets of using *détente* to promote world revolution and claimed that 'they reserve the right unto themselves to commit any crime, to lie, [and] to cheat'. Later, in 1981, he attributed all the unrest in the world to the Soviet Union and in 1983 delivered his infamous 'evil empire' speech. This potent combination of paranoia and moralism was particularly evident in his attitudes toward Central America. Alarmist assessments of Soviet intentions were 'emotional and so lacking in factual support that it invited accusations of disingenuousness',[10] yet falling dominoes were nevertheless revisited and the communist advance portrayed as a challenge to Manifest Destiny.

Beyond this, Reagan's containment policy was an awkward and inconsistent 'pick and mix' of previous strategies as he attempted to reconcile a renewed messianic globalism with the debilitating 'Vietnam Syndrome' and the pragmatic constraints of the 1980s, such as alliance attitudes and the relative decline of US power. His militarisation of containment smacked heavily of NSC-68; but it was ironic that an otherwise fiscally conservative Republican administration was prepared to fund rearmament through massive deficit spending. Whilst US foreign aid was slashed, Reagan embarked upon the most rapid increase in defence spending in US peacetime history. He launched a five-year $180 billion programme to modernise US strategic forces. He reversed Carter's cancellation of the B-1 bomber, approved a 600–ship navy, stepped up preparations to deploy Pershing II missiles in Western Europe, and announced SDI, which threatened MAD by potentially giving the US a safe first-strike capability. In his first three years, Reagan increased defence expenditure by 40% in real terms and by 1985 the US was spending $300 billion per annum on defence.

Reagan's general perspective on containment, however, was reminiscent of Eisenhower's. He returned to Dulles' themes of 'liberation' and 'roll-back', but was even more ambitious. The Soviet system was in economic crisis and, by taking the initiative, the US could add to its distress. Some hoped to cripple it via a new arms race. Others looked to 'roll-back' communism in the Third World and in this they had some success because, while their view of containment was global, they were generally careful about the extent and nature of their commitment, despite their wild rhetoric.

In light of the Vietnam legacy, US troops were used sparingly, especially after the slaughter of US marines in the Lebanon in 1983. Thereafter, they were restricted to actions such as the overthrow in October 1983 of the marxist government on Grenada. Much more use was made of the counterinsurgency operations popularised by Kennedy, of the proxies favoured by Nixon, and of the covert operations which had been the penchant of Eisenhower. The CIA budget soared and the administration frequently shielded its funds and activities from congressional scrutiny. For example, it controlled much of the $2 billion given to El Salvador between 1980 and 1985, was integrally involved in organising the Nicaraguan Contras, and had extensive dealings with General Noriega in Panama. The US also funded its proxies generously. In 1985, $250–300 million went to Afghan rebels and $15 million to the anti-communist force, UNITA, in Angola. By 1987, the Nicaraguan Contras had received $100 million, non-communist resistance groups in Kampuchea $20 million, and anti-marxist groups in Ethiopia over $0.5 million.

Paradoxically, at the same time that Reagan rearmed, pursued roll-back in the Third World and postured aggressively *vis-à-vis* the Soviets, he also moved towards *détente*. Whereas the NSC-68 elite interpreted negotiation from strength as entailing Soviet capitulation, Reagan was more flexible. Some have suggested that the vitriol of his first years in office was designed to construct the domestic political base necessary to enable lasting *détente*.[11] Although this attributes to Reagan both a questionable prescience and a dubious long-termism, there is little doubt that he was more liberal than many of his advisers and possessed of a strong distaste of nuclear defences. He encouraged trade with the Soviet Union, notably in September 1983 when he concluded the biggest grain deal ever, but it was nuclear weaponry that became the centrepiece of his quest for East–West political accommodation. Early efforts focused on an Intermediate Nuclear Force (INF) treaty and the so-called 'zero option' – no deployments of cruise and Pershing missiles in Europe in return for USSR withdrawal of its SS-20s. This would have so disadvantaged the Soviets that it has often been seen as a tactic simultaneously to rearm and score 'peace points' with nervous allies and against the Kremlin. Nevertheless, after Soviet–American relations reached their lowest ebb in 1983 since the Cuban missile crisis, Reagan transformed arms limitation to arms reduction talks and re-launched *détente* with an announcement in late 1984 of new talks linking INF, START, and weapons in space.

Ultimately Reagan's version of *détente,* due to a combination of mutual interest and personal diplomacy, produced greater results than did US initiatives in the 1970s. In Mikhail Gorbachev, who became General Secretary of the Soviet Union in March 1985, Reagan found a partner in leadership. On a personal level the two shared a penchant for personal summitry and established a rapport, particularly at their meeting in October 1986 in Reykjavik, which mellowed the Cold War atmosphere. Even more importantly, they had a coincidence of interest in relaxing East–West tensions. Reagan was resigned to the 'long haul' but keen nevertheless to be seen as proactive, rather than simply responding to Soviet policies. Gorbachev needed a period of respite during which to restructure the Soviet economy in a way that allowed sustainable development, particularly in terms of tackling inefficiency and balancing military expenditure against consumer demand. As a result, Reagan and Gorbachev held four crucial summits between 1985 and 1988 that helped change the course of the Cold War. A new sense of optimism permeated superpower exchanges and was reflected in groundbreaking agreements, such as an INF treaty in December 1987 that provided for the destruction of an entire category of nuclear missiles.[12]

Bush and the end of the Cold War

In 1989, George Bush succeeded Reagan. An unenviable task awaited him. President Bush lacked Reagan's charisma and ability to disguise the deep contradictions within US foreign policy. He also inherited problems that ranged from economic recession to significant discontent amidst NATO allies, despite the close relationship that had existed between Reagan and Britain's Margaret Thatcher. Furthermore, Bush faced a Cold War that differed markedly from that of the hostile, yet relatively easily managed, situation of the early 1980s. In January 1987, Gorbachev launched *perestroika,* and between 1988 and 1990 the Soviets made dramatic unilateral cuts in their forces in Europe. Also, throughout the first half of 1989, the Bush administration was regaled with reports of Soviet economic weakness and discontent among their satellites. This highlighted a critical question that had arisen during the later Reagan years: was the Soviet Union undergoing lasting change or was Gorbachev restructuring with a view to resurgent power and renewed superpower confrontation? Moreover, as reforms seemed to spiral out of control, a fascinating new factor was added to the equation. As Secretary of State James Baker put it, 'What happens if Gorbachev loses, if things go to hell in a handbasket over there?'[13] In other words, would the end of the Cold War really be a victory for the US or the precursor to something much worse?

Bush's initial proclamations suggested that he was ready to adapt US foreign policy to suit the changing times. On 12 May 1989, he talked of moving beyond containment to a policy of integration, whereby the Soviet Union would be brought into the community of nations. Indeed, standing at the confluence between Cold War and 'New World Order', Bush had a plethora of options. He could pursue roll-back in the Third World with far greater expectations of success than those harboured by Eisenhower and even Reagan. He could capitalise on the Reagan–Gorbachev dynamic and take *détente* to heights unimagined by Nixon and Kissinger. Or he could meaningfully challenge Soviet power in Eastern Europe.

However, Bush's promises of integration were soon exposed for what they were, empty rhetoric. Staunchly conservative, Bush had already resolved privately upon a much less inspiring course. He disparaged the 'vision thing' and feared that, if he capitalised upon Gorbachev's weakness and challenged communist power in Eastern Europe, he might bolster Soviet hardliners or generate systemic weakness with unpredictable consequences, or possibly do both. Consequently, in April 1989 he accepted a passive policy of 'status quo plus'. This consisted of broadening the superpower dialogue at the same time as slowing the momentum created by the Reagan–Gorbachev dynamic, which was considered to have raised unrealistic and dangerous expectations. In 1990, Bush was pushed into a slightly more expansive policy by massive domestic and international pressure. The unimaginative 'status quo plus' was replaced by a slightly more optimistic approach based upon five objectives: to encourage Gorbachev's reforms; to maintain the territorial integrity of the USSR; to conclude arms controls favourable to the US lest Gorbachev be replaced by hardliners; to ensure that a reunified Germany obtain NATO and EC membership; and to achieve a stable and democratic Eastern Europe.[14] Nevertheless, rather than being assertive in the pursuit of these objectives, Bush's subsequent foreign policy remained largely reactive to events.

The Bush approach to containment had merits. It is all too easy to use hindsight to criticise a pragmatic, cautious policy that was evolved in turbulent times. Unsure of Soviet motives and objectives, it made sense for Bush to require Gorbachev to pass various tests of commitment to *perestroika*. These included liberalisation of Central and Eastern Europe and renunciation of the Brezhnev Doctrine (promulgated in 1968 and claiming Soviet rights to intervene in the affairs of socialist states). Bush also capitalised upon Soviet weakness. He took vigorous unilateral action against Panama in December 1989 and led the 1990–91 military intervention in the Gulf against Iraq. Furthermore, once 'Gorby sceptics' such as Defence Secretary Richard Cheney had been silenced, Bush took the logical step of re-engaging the Soviet Union as a partner in stability. Bush met Gorbachev for the first time in December 1989 in Malta and thereafter moved to bolster the USSR and underwrite the reform process. Tied aid was used to push the Soviet Union into further reforms. MFN trading status was eventually granted, packages were developed to help with market reform, and promises made about developments in arms control verification. Significant progress was also made on disarmament. NATO and Warsaw Pact leaders concluded a treaty on conventional force levels in Europe (CFE) in 1990 and the START treaty was signed at the Moscow summit in July 1991. And at Camp David in 1990 a momentous agreement was reached when Gorbachev accepted the 'two plus four' arrangement[15] that allowed a reunified Germany to be brought into NATO.

Bush pragmatism, though, exacted a high moral and practical price. It revealed more painful contradictions of US foreign policy as Bush took containment to the opposite end of the spectrum from whence it had started. Whereas Truman had looked to contain Soviet strength and achieve outright victory, Bush decided that US interests lay in preventing outright victory and containing Soviet weakness. The US had to prop up the 'evil empire' in the dual hope of maintaining stability and that the Soviet Union would reform itself in a way acceptable to the West. Unsurprisingly, this threw up all sorts of other unpalatable contradictions too. For example, when Lithuania declared independence in March 1990, Bush, to help Gorbachev, tolerated Soviet intimidation of the breakaway republic and delayed recognition of it until September 1991. Similarly, he did his best in August 1991 to cool Ukrainian demands for secession. This casts in sharp relief the contrast between Bush's promises of freedom and 'integration' and his actions in Eastern Europe. In some ways the hypocrisy of Bush's statecraft is of little surprise for his predecessors had all done likewise in deference to wider US containment objectives. However, there can be few ironies more bitter than that which saw Bush abandon the freedom of others in order to support the very regime that denied them their freedom and that forty years previously the US had vowed to destroy.

Bush's wait-and-see approach also surrendered the Cold War initiative taken by Reagan, undermined American leadership, and condemned the US to the role of passive spectator as the Cold War collapsed around it. Indeed, insofar as Bush's belated policy of engagement saved neither Gorbachev nor system stability, the Cold War ended despite American policy. Instead, the catalyst came from Europe in the form of Chancellor Kohl, who forced the issue of German reunification. In February 1990, he pushed for reunification by the end of the year. Ultimately, a beleaguered Gorbachev was unable to refuse. On 3 October, Germany was reunified, the Soviet Union was in freefall, and the Cold War was effectively over.

Since that time, debate has raged as to how much credit to give to Reagan and his policies for bringing about the end of the Cold War. Did his hard-line rhetoric and massive rearmament force the Soviets into an unsustainable and ultimately disastrous arms race? Was his meaningful negotiation from strength the key to unlocking superpower antagonism? Did Western Europe's own form of *détente* with the East, grave strains within NATO, and the burgeoning anti-nuclear movement force moderation upon his second term? Or was American policy a relatively minor factor in Soviet collapse compared to structural economic problems, onerous commitments such as Afghanistan – the Soviet Union's Vietnam – and an over-extension in the Third World which eventually saw it, as well as the US, challenged as imperialist? History is, after all, littered with the rise and decline of such empires.

This debate will go on as more information becomes available, but what is certain is that neither Reagan nor Bush was any more able than their predecessors to make containment work coherently. First, key enabling factors were missing. Reagan never instilled into the Second Cold War the American commitment and leadership that characterised the first. Key allies, notably in Western Europe, came to see the US, rather than the USSR, as the more likely cause of conflict and disagreed sharply with Reagan's policies in the Middle East, Central America, and with the bombing raid on 'terrorist' Libya in 1986. The American people and Congress, too, were sufficiently divided that Reagan could neither exorcise the ghosts of Vietnam nor re-establish the imperial presidency, as the Iran–Contra scandal demonstrated in 1986–87. Second, American means palpably could not meet the return to global containment.

'Reaganomics' transformed the US from the world's major creditor in 1981 to its largest debtor and, with the Wall Street crash of October 1987, ushered in a new recession. Third, Reagan's moralism *vis-à-vis* the Soviets and their interference in other states contrasted sharply with his own extensive use of covert operations, gunboat diplomacy in Grenada, and support for undemocratic and brutal regimes, such as in El Salvador. Public attempts to square this long-standing and damaging circle simply heaped ridicule upon the administration. In March 1981, Secretary of State Alexander Haig labelled as terrorists all revolutionaries except those fighting communism, and the US Ambassador to the UN, Jeanne Kirkpatrick, famously distinguished between authoritarian dictatorships which were friendly to the US and capable of evolving into democracies, and left-wing totalitarian dictatorships which were not. Finally Bush, as he dealt with the twilight of Cold War, revealed two of the great ironies of post-war US foreign policy. First, like other self-proclaimed champions of the Free World who preceded him, he sacrificed the rights of the peoples of Central and Eastern Europe to Cold War priorities, albeit this time bizarrely to support rather than undermine the USSR. Second, Bush's passivity demonstrated that forty years of containment had socialised the US to such an extent that it had greater interests in the *status quo* than in actively seeking an end to the Cold War.[16]

Conclusion

At considerable cost of lives and US constitutional and political virtue, containment helped to maintain the integrity of the Free World against the communist challenge. That containment endured throughout the Cold War as the guiding principle of US foreign policy is, in one sense, surprising because, however it was formulated, it was replete with contradictions, blinding oversimplifications, and frighteningly rigid prescriptions. Yet, it was not a strategy but many strategies that evolved in accordance with the interplay between perceptions of policy-makers, variables in the international system, and domestic politics. Some even argue that it was not a strategy at all but rather a general statement of intent, a clarion call to action, or a convenient catchphrase which justified the expansion of American interests in a post-colonial world by whatever means policy-makers thought necessary. As Secretary of State Dean Acheson testified long after the event, NSC-68 was designed to 'bludgeon' the mass mind of top government into allowing Truman to make a decision and be able to carry it through. What is certain, though, is that for two principal reasons the debate about containment will continue. First, its importance and effectiveness as a means of regulating and then, ultimately, ending the Cold War will be tested by historians as archival material becomes available from both East and West. Second, containment was as nebulous as it was simplistic. It could be, and was, used as justification for almost any American action or non-action, often with seemingly little relevance to Cold War issues. Consequently, writers of different genres and political persuasion have almost limitless scope for interpretation.

4   Economic statecraft

US foreign economic policy has prompted fiercely contested debates. Liberals see US capitalism as flawed, but benign and progressive, while New Left historians and world systems theorists see it as an aggressive force, which ruthlessly exploits other countries. Paul Kennedy discerns a dangerous pattern of US relative economic decline since the Second World War: Joseph Nye does not. Stephen Gill sees a form of supranational capitalism emerging with hegemonic control of the world emanating primarily from US corporations and the capitalist ethos that permeates Washington. Others, like Susan Strange, assert that an international political economy exists, which challenges both traditional distinctions between security and economic concerns and state-centric analyses of international relations. Strange sees states functioning in an interpenetrated and economically interdependent world, where one not only needs to concentrate on military security, but also on production, financial and knowledge structures. If even part of this analysis is accepted, it more than justifies our present concern with economic aspects of US foreign policy.[1]

Facts, figures and motives

If one were to compile seven wonders of the twentieth century, US economic performance in the Second World War would be one of them. The figures are staggering. Gross domestic production (GDP) rose from $88.6 billion in 1939 to $135 billion in 1945. At the war's end, the US held $20 billion of the world's $33 billion of gold reserves. It made half of the world's goods, had over half of the world's shipping, provided one third of the world's exports and carried over 73% of the world's combined domestic and international airline passengers. The US was an economic colossus, but an important factor for foreign policy analysis needs to be borne in mind here: the vast proportion of all this was produced and consumed domestically. More than any other major economy, the US had enormous self-sufficiency. Not until the 1960s did imports and exports become quantitatively significant in the GDP. Between 1960–88 exports as a percentage of GDP rose from 5.2% to 11.4% and imports rose from 4.7% to 9.7%; by 1997 exports and imports combined were equivalent to 25% of US GDP. On the basis of this late development of import/export significance for US prosperity, it could be argued that the large cost of US foreign economic policy must have been justified by security rather than economic considerations. This sounds persuasive, but it misses some important points.

The US entered the international economy in a massive way after the Second World War because of an inextricable mixture of concerns about security and economic prosperity. In the 1930s, liberals had changed the architecture of capitalism in the US by making its face more humane, by introducing regulatory management structures, and by making it more accountable to the people. This was the New Deal. During the war, President Roosevelt and his advisers decided that the New Deal vision needed to be internationalised, with the US at the centre of management. There were six key ideas behind this. First, economic discrimination had to end because it caused friction and war. Second, a free-market would bring global prosperity. Third, Americans needed new markets abroad to help absorb the enormous productive capacity of the US, otherwise there would be another economic depression. Fourth, although the US was less dependent on imports and exports than any other major power, it was, nevertheless, short of several strategic commodities such as oil, bauxite, rubber, tungsten and uranium. Fifth, there were foreign profits to be made for US capitalism. And sixth, establishing a strong institutionalised position for itself in the management of the international economy would facilitate the exercise of US power, for good or ill, in the foreign domain. For this broad array of reasons, rather than as a result of the uni-causal capitalist dynamic often used by New Left historians, the US moulded and then managed a new liberal economic world order.

Management of the world economy 1945–73

It is important to note that official government policy was not popular everywhere in the US. Its distinguished tradition of protectionism was potent enough to prevent the ITO being ratified by Congress and so the world had to make do with the GATT from 1948 until the inception of the World Trade Organisation (WTO) in January 1995. US protectionism waxed and waned continually throughout the post-war period and should not be dismissed as a spent force.

Multilateralism, the key concept in the IMF and the GATT, facilitated the operation of international capitalism. The IMF, through the Bretton Woods system, made all currencies freely convertible into each other at rates pegged to the dollar whose value was fixed at $35 per fine ounce of gold. And the GATT reduced tariff barriers through the principles of reciprocity and MFN. For example, Britain would reduce the tariff on imports of US planes in return for a US reduction on British jewellery (reciprocity) and then these new tariff rates would be extended to all other members of the GATT (MFN). However, the GATT, while a facilitator of tariff reductions on manufactured goods, was not effective in the agricultural realm, exempted service industries and regional economic groupings from its brief, and had ineffective enforcement powers. Nevertheless, through the operation of the GATT and the IMF, the US hoped for freer trade and for the US dollar to become supreme in the monetary system.

American multilateralism was never pure. It was shot through with self-serving exceptions in the agriculture sector, in the airline and maritime industries and even in the GATT, where the Americans rejected the idea of across-the-board tariff reductions in favour of reciprocity and MFN. With these procedures they could use their economic strength to more effective advantage. The US had privileged management positions in all the institutions set up to manage the new economic world order. No organisation, until the creation of the WTO, could make policy without US consent because of its veto power. Throughout, idealistic principles were clearly modified in favour of realist American calculations of self-interest.

The US hoped that their new universal economic order could be implemented speedily after the war. That hope was dashed because the Soviets refused to participate, the economies of Western Europe were not fit enough to play the game, and the Cold War imposed new priorities. Economic disorder in Western Europe and the imperative of fostering a speedy recovery, in order to inoculate it against the spread of communism, led the Americans to adopt regionalism, and that compromised their multilateralism further because regionalism discriminates against outsiders. They pumped $12 billion of Marshall Aid into Western Europe, encouraged integration, and tolerated preferential tariffs and currency controls, which discriminated against US exporters. Bretton Woods was partially suspended and the GATT, after substantial cuts in tariffs in 1947, lay largely dormant until the 1960s. The US accepted these costs mainly for the sake of immediate security priorities, but they hoped that regionalism would be an effective midwife for multilateralism.

At the end of the 1950s, general convertibility was finally delivered:

rules and to emulate OPEC's success by forming cartels to raise commodity prices. They also demanded more credit, aid, and management power in institutions such as the IMF. At the same time, there were linked and growing criticisms of the operation of Western MNCs for exploiting the Lesser Developed Countries (LDCs), for distorting their economic growth, and for creating an alienated clientele class often comprised of ex-patriots and supportive of corrupt, authoritarian local regimes.

These demands and criticisms came at a bad time for Washington. Already troubled by recession, President Gerald Ford saw the NIEO as unacceptable socialist demands for a redistribution of the world's wealth. The most robust of US responses to these developments came in 1975 when Secretary of State Kissinger warned OPEC that the US would not tolerate oil prices rising to such an extent that they fundamentally threatened Western economies. Successive administrations also rejected criticisms of MNCs and defended them both for bringing employment, investment and development and as a means for the international dissemination of technology and efficient production techniques. Such defences sounded hollow in Guatemala and Chile, where coups in 1954 and 1973 respectively had been, at least partially, organised with the help of US companies. During the 1980s, the unity of the non-aligned countries gave way to schisms. OPEC became less effective as the West developed alternative power and oil sources, and some countries, such as the Asian Tigers – Singapore, Hong Kong, South Korea and Taiwan – and LDCs, such as Brazil, developed interests more compatible with the advanced Western countries as they emerged from underdevelopment. This further compromised the unity of the Group of 77. In retrospect, it was all a bit like trying to square the circle, expecting the weak to prevail against the strong.

The empire strikes back

At the management level of world capitalism, President Carter and his Secretary of State Cyrus Vance tried to resurrect some order through a series of economic summits of the seven leading industrial countries (G7), which aimed to co-ordinate national policies in a mutually helpful way. In particular, they strove to persuade West Germany and Japan to stimulate recovery by re-inflating their economies, but with little success. In 1979, the overthrow of the Shah of Iran by revolutionary Moslem fundamentalists sparked off a new oil crisis, which re-ignited inflation in the West and led to further economic disarray and recession.

Entering office in 1981, President Reagan looked to the free market for solutions. He adopted aggressive unilateral policies to deal with trade issues and developed domestic economic policy in contradictory ways, which had negative effects on the world economy. Reagan rejected Keynesianism, cut taxes, raised interest rates to squeeze out inflation, but increased government spending massively on rearmament, as a key strategy in the Second Cold War. These policies fostered a consumer-led recovery, fed largely by foreign imports. The impact on the international economy was substantial. High interest rates for the dollar, which remained the dominant international currency despite US economic problems, sucked in massive amounts of foreign investment, which in turn helped to offset the impact of the enormous US trade deficit. These developments made the international economy more volatile and created a tendency for damagingly high interest rates elsewhere. The hardest hit were Third World countries, which accumulated massive service payments on dollar debts. This precipitated a crisis throughout the international economy. In 1982, Mexico announced that it could not service its debts of $80 billion and by 1990 total LDC debts stood at $1.3 trillion. Catastrophe was averted by re-scheduling, writing down and cancelling debts, and by offering new aid.

This economic volatility brought forth some new initiatives. Hoping to build on the success of the Tokyo GATT talks, 1973–79, the US pushed for what became the Uruguay round 1986–93. In international monetary matters, the Europeans took an initiative in 1978 and produced the European Monetary System in their quest for stability. At the Plaza Hotel in New York in 1985, the US followed their example and agreed with Japan, Britain, France and West Germany to seek more co-ordinated efforts in international economic policy, especially in monetary exchange matters. In the following year, Canada and Italy joined them.

Clearly, the US had not abandoned multilateralism, but this was not its only line of policy. Unilateralism, aggressive deregulation in industries where the US could benefit (such as the airline industry), and moves towards regionalism and protectionism were all part and parcel of policy during the 1980s. To many, these contradictory strategies seemed to be symptomatic of hegemonic decline. Now the US felt obliged to pursue its own national economic interests in the best way it could. Sometimes this would mean multilateral liberalism, at other times regionalism or even protectionism. With the end of the Cold War the temptation to pursue US national economic interests, even at the expense of friends and allies, became irresistible. President Clinton entered office in 1993 with a determination to give priority to economic policy, not just in the domestic, but in the international realm as well.

After the Cold War

With no immediate traditional kind of security challenge, the US foreign affairs agenda changed. Military security was still an issue, but one among several that vied for attention and priority. This resulted in a more open and partisan political debate, which involved domestic constituencies both directly and through congressional representation. Often at the centre of this were economic issues: by the mid-1990s US exports and imports combined amounted to 25% of US GDP, there were continuing worries about US decline, and there was a massive balance of trade deficit. During the election campaign, Clinton had recognised President Bush's failure to identify the importance of economic policy: once in office, he strove to correct things.

Clinton elevated economics to high policy with the creation of the NEC and the appointment of Rubin as its director. He also used Mickey Kantor and Charlene Barshefsky, successively USTRs, to promote trade. The USTR had aggressively attacked reprobate trade partners since 1985, by which time it was clear that non-tariff barriers were key issues in world trade. The US negotiated a large number of voluntary export restraint agreements (VERs), to limit the flood of exports from Japan, the EC, and the newly emerging economies of the world. These agreements were voluntary in name alone: they were backed by aggressive diplomacy and threats of retaliation if they were not accepted and complied with. The US was also unhappy with barriers to service industries, not covered by the GATT, where it felt it would have competitive advantages in a freer market. This campaign became even more aggressive in the 1990s. Clinton also encouraged the US Treasury and the Commerce Department to adopt higher profiles. His first Secretary of Commerce, Ron Brown, introduced a National Export Strategy and the Big Emerging Markets Program in order to promote exports. The 1994 State Department International Affairs Budget made commitments to building democracy and promoting peace, but much of the agenda was economic: promoting economic growth and sustainable development; addressing global problems and providing humanitarian assistance.

With the agenda set and the institutional context prepared, Clinton moved vigorously, though not always with consistent policies. In November 1993, he called a conference in Seattle of the Asian Pacific Economic Co-operation (APEC) forum, which made pledges on free trade. That same year NAFTA was approved by the US, Mexico and Canada, and came into operation on 1 January 1994. At the same time, the US took unilateral action through Section 301 legislation of the 1988 Omnibus Trade and Competitiveness Act to counter unacceptable trade practices by other countries, regardless of whether or not the action fell within the rules of GATT. In 1995 and 1996 this nearly resulted in a trade war with China (a non-GATT member) over video and technological pirating. Kantor and Barshefsky successively threatened retaliatory tariffs and the Chinese backed down at the last minute on each occasion. Despite this unilateralism, which directly challenged the ethos of the GATT, the US still promoted GATT's development, ratified both the outcome of the Uruguay round and the creation of the WTO, and at the end of the decade welcomed China's membership. In December 1994, Clinton hosted a Hemispheric Summit in Miami, which committed all members (except Cuba) to a Free Trade Area for the Americas. This was to be developed by expanding NAFTA, and Chile was singled out as the next potential member. These were significant and important achievements, but there had also been developments which began to unsettle US economic policy and expose some of its contradictions.

Economics in the post-Cold War world were accorded higher priority than before, but political and strategic matters still influenced economic policy-making, as did a growing impact from domestic isolationism and protectionism. In 1994, the Republicans swept to victory in the mid-term elections. Their control of both houses of Congress and their Contract with America programme, designed to cut spending and end the Federal deficit, meant increased political pressures which fragmented economic policy and exacerbated existing contradictions. Clinton was unable to repeat the successes of his first term after his re-election in 1996. Renewed criticisms of NAFTA prevented its enlargement and freer trade goals within APEC were put on hold. The overall picture of the 1990s is thus even more confused and contradictory than the 1980s.

In his State of the Union Message on 19 January 1999, President Clinton declared: 'I issue a call to the nations of the world to join the United States in a new round of global negotiations to expand exports … We must tear down barriers, open markets and expand trade.'[4] A clear enough policy one might think. And yet, with a visible trade gap of $244 billion in the year up to the previous November and lacking 'fast track' authority because of congressional opposition, the prospects for achieving trade liberalisation were not good. In fact, in that same State of the Union Message, Clinton threatened retaliation against Japan for sending a flood of cheap steel to the US. A few days later, the Administration's declarations about reviving Section 301 legislation received rapturous support, and in March 1999 the US refused to wait for further WTO action on a banana dispute with the EU and slapped punitive duties on what seemed to be a random selection of European exports. Regionalism and unilateralism, evident in various guises in US foreign economic policy, signified to some a more inward looking, a more protectionist, and a more isolationist US that cared less for the economic health of others than it had done in the past. By the mid-1990s, the US had already become the most miserly of all industrial nations in terms of its development aid. It stood at a meagre 0.01% of the US GNP. In absolute terms this was $7.4 billion, but much of that went to Israel and Egypt, and the figure ranked behind that given by Japan, France and Germany.

All this was happening as the US economy flourished. Many pondered on what might happen once it faltered. With sustained growth for over eight years, unemployment and inflation down and GDP growth running at 4%, some talked of a Second American Century. But, with protectionism and contradictions growing in US foreign economic policy, the key question is what would this Second American Century look like? Answers to that question became even more difficult at the end of 1999 when the WTO conference in Seattle was besieged by demonstrators protesting in ways reminiscent of the disillusionment with capitalism of the 1960s.

Conclusion

While US foreign policy successfully resisted demands for a more equitable world economic order in the 1970s, it came under renewed attack at the end of the millennium and it had failed to conjure up a new economic world order to replace the one that had collapsed in 1973. In the field of monetary exchange there was more reliance on the market to decide value, but moderated by G7 after 1985, and by European monetary union after 1998. In trade, the US vigorously promoted deregulation, such as in the airline industry, where it provided self-advantage. It adopted unilateral forms of protection, such as VERs and Section 301 legislation, on the grounds that these were simply retaliation for bad practices elsewhere. It moved away from multilateralism with the creation of NAFTA, yet it continued to encourage multilateralism through the WTO when it suited. The foreign economic agenda had been elevated to high politics after the end of the Cold War, but political and strategic considerations continued their influence, albeit at a lower level for the time being. Having been elevated to high politics, economic statecraft also became subject to more influence from Congress and domestic constituencies. Partisanship and ideology both made their mark and foreign economic policy became difficult to formulate. Thus the key questions for the future are: To what extent is this pragmatic pursuit of a mosaic of often contradictory policies likely to continue? Might it be here for good, or will a clearer, more consistent policy emerge to guide the world to a new and less turbulent economic anchorage?

5 The US and Europe, 1950–89

Beware your allies?

Was containment in Europe a success, a failure, or a misreading of key European dynamics? How accurate is it to talk of US hegemony or even empire in Europe, be it the constructs of neo-marxist economic determinism or voluntaristic forms, such as Geir Lundestad's 'empire by integration/invitation' and Charles S. Maier's 'analog of empire'?[1] Whatever the answers, it is clear that after 1950 Western Europe was a difficult theatre for US policy-makers. 'Inconvenient' leaders could not be toppled, nor client states built, nor economic aid determine outcomes decisively. Rather, Europe was the home of long-established states who were both America's key allies and disturbingly prone to regard the Cold War as an important but secondary issue next to their defence of established interests, their adjustment to a post-colonial world, and their post-war battle with economic globalisation. Ironically, it was the US that helped to put these states back on the path to stability after the damage of the Second World War through Marshall Aid and security guarantees sufficient to underwrite the West European integration process.

The nature of the problem

By 1950, Europe was probably the easiest place to wage containment. With the notable exceptions of Franco's Spain and Salazar's Portugal, the US could deal with countries where liberal democracy, capitalism, and 'suitable' religions were well-established. Nor did the US have to make difficult decisions about political shades of revolutionary nationalist movements. Also, the line between East and West was drawn clearly, a stark contrast to the situation in the jungles of Asia and the conflict-strewn Middle East. Marshall Aid effectively divided Europe into two blocs and helped to consolidate Western Europe sufficiently to repel the communist threat. This divide was institutionalised after the Berlin Blockade in 1948, which irrevocably split the city between the East and West so long as the Cold War existed. Thereafter, through the creation of

NATO in 1949 and the Warsaw Pact in 1955, both sides consolidated beyond realistic challenge the informal division of Europe drawn by Marshall Aid (the only exception was the case of Tito's Yugoslavia). For example, despite lofty US rhetoric about 'roll-back', no-one seriously believed that anything could, or should, be done when the Soviets intervened in Hungary in 1956 and in Czechoslovakia in 1968.

Throughout the remainder of the Cold War only the recurring issue of Berlin caused major East–West tension in Europe, and even this was settled without a 'loss' to either superpower. West Germany was the linchpin of American policy in Europe because its geostrategic position, manpower and economy were vital to containing communism and because NATO had based its forward defence strategy on the River Elbe, the eastern border of West Germany. The great fear after the resolution of the Berlin Blockade was that the Soviets would woo West Germany into neutrality in return for reunification. Matters came to a head when this deal was implicitly offered to Bonn through the 1957 Rapacki Plan and when Krushchev followed up with an ultimatum in November 1958. Either the West entered talks within six months over Germany or Krushchev would conclude a separate peace treaty and transfer East Berlin to East German control. Eighteen months of intermittent parleying between Eisenhower and Krushchev succeeded only in souring their relationship, particularly when an American U-2 spy plane was brought down deep over Soviet territory in May 1960 and caused a complete debacle at the Paris US–Soviet summit. Eventually, Krushchev settled the issue of Berlin *de facto* by building the Wall, and in September 1971 Russia and the West formally acknowledged the division of Berlin, with the Western sector linked to, but constitutionally separate from, West Germany.[2]

Why then did Europe, as a zone of genuine stability, give the US such difficulty during the Cold War? The answer lies very much in the question of control, or more precisely the fear of having an insufficiency of it. Europe was historically divided, Franco-German rivalry had been the focal point of two world wars, and when the Cold War developed Europe was again the front line. Also, there were different types of nation-state there, each with different preoccupations. France and Britain were colonial powers with a global outlook. West Germany was an artificially divided country which, whilst seeking re-acceptance into the international arena, undoubtedly harboured desires for reunification. Spain was under Franco's fascist dictatorship, communist revolt in Greece had been the trigger for the Truman Doctrine, and there was a strong possibility that vulnerable states might declare neutrality, as Austria did when Krushchev pulled the Red Army out in May 1955.

Another very important problem, which caused the US grave difficulties in the Atlantic alliance and the Third World, was that it could not deal with the European powers in isolation from the rest of the world. For example, the geostrategic importance of Greece and Turkey persuaded the US to bring both within the NATO structure in 1952. Once there, though, they continued their long-running battle over Cyprus. Even more problematic was the relationship with Europe's two leading colonial powers. The US expected Britain and France to rearm massively, to maintain their European and overseas commitments, and from their colonial possessions to provide bases for US use. However, at the same time, it spewed forth anti-colonial sentiment in an attempt to ally itself with the forces of Third World nationalism and criticised its colonial allies if they failed or refused benevolently to guide their colonies through to stable independence. As a result, the Americans frequently antagonised their colonial and Third World allies. They also often inherited the problems left behind when their West European allies withdrew from their colonial possessions. The most infamous example of this was Vietnam.

From reconstruction to refusal

US policy towards Europe had to overcome historic divisions and evolve in tandem with global containment. For example, US assistance in the early 1950s to France in its fight against communism in Indo-China was also geared to securing its support for West German rearmament through the European Defence Community (EDC). Likewise, the US had to balance the Anglo–American Special Relationship against its specific designs for Europe because Britain, due to its colonial possessions, prestige and military and economic power, was America's foremost partner in both global containment and management of the Bretton Woods system.[3] However, the principal way American policy-makers sought to hold West Europe together was by pushing for its integration in the belief that this would be the most efficient way of economically reviving it. It would also contain Germany and the USSR, develop a sense of collective interest amongst the states, allow America to reduce commitments to Europe, and secure US access to essential markets. Consequently, the Americans abandoned temporarily their drive for multilateralism in favour of nurturing European regional integration.

Europe needed American economic aid desperately to rebuild its wartorn economies, to resist communist subversion, and to redefine its international relationships. The Americans used this as leverage to 'remake Europe in an American mode.'[4] The ERP required West European states to administer US funds collectively and on a regional basis. The Americans also encouraged European federalists, supported the 1948 Hague Conference, and endorsed the proposal of Jean Monnet, head of the French economic modernisation programme, for a European Coal and Steel Community (ECSC). Monnet's suggestion held particular appeal because it would put the essential ingredients for war-making under supranational control, bind the Federal Republic of Germany to the West, and help with Franco-German reconciliation.

In April 1951, the Treaty of Paris established the ECSC, involving West Germany, France, Italy and Benelux. It seemed that US ambitions were being realised. However, was this really the case? There was some American inconsistency about integration and, despite the scale of their investment, they could not always influence decisively their allies' policies. For example, the Americans became uncertain about whether they wanted Britain integrated into Europe and, while Britain co-operated sufficiently to establish the European Payments Union, it refused to compromise its sovereignty by entering the ECSC.[5] It also undercut US ambitions for European integration by pushing successfully the inter-governmental Organisation for European Economic Co-operation to administer Marshall Aid. The French, too, blocked key US initiatives. On 12 September 1950, Secretary of State Acheson dropped 'the bomb at the Waldorf': West Germany had to be rearmed within NATO to the tune of ten divisions because of the increased military demands created by the globalisation of containment. France objected and proposed instead the Pleven Plan for a supranational European army that would limit the development of a German sense of military identity. The Americans were not keen but eventually supported it because they could not force an alternative. When the EDC was slow to materialise, Dulles delivered his famous 'agonising reappraisal' warning of possible US withdrawal from Europe if the EDC failed. However, even this could not force the Europeans into line. In 1954, the French rejected their own plan, a decision facilitated by the fact that American leverage *vis-à-vis* Paris had by this time been reduced by the end of the Korean War and French withdrawal from Indo-China, where they had relied heavily on American aid. Ultimately, France sanctioned what it had rejected in 1950, the integration of German troops into Western defence. This was done by extending the 1948 Brussels Treaty to Italy and West Germany to form the Western European Union, and by substantial British military commitments to continental Europe. By this time, though, the Eisenhower administration had clearly suffered setbacks in its European policy and unity within NATO seemed little more than skin deep. Indeed, it was clear that while no state questioned US military predominance, American leadership would be sorely tried whenever it ran up against European national interests and whenever East–West tensions diminished.[6]

1955–70: the American 'awakening'

Between 1955 and 1970 American policy-makers had to revise key assumptions, especially about the complementary nature of US–West European interests. Three key threats confronted them: US relative economic decline, fears of a West German rapprochement with the USSR, and General de Gaulle's vision of a French-led Western Europe which would be an independent 'third force' between the superpowers. Ironically, the challenge from the East, which centred on Berlin, was quickly settled by the building of the Wall. However, this actually fed American fears about the interlinked challenges of Western Europe's growing economic strength and de Gaulle's ability to hijack the integration process for French ends.

American influence was declining because the US economy had begun to falter under the burden of containment and the economic challenge from Japan and Europe. For example, in 1958–59 the US payments deficit increased markedly, 1960 witnessed the first run on the dollar, and foreign holdings of dollars exceeded the US gold reserve for the first time. Moreover, de Gaulle's hand had been strengthened in three ways. First, Bonn, uneasy about US weakness over Berlin and its exclusion from nuclear technology, sought to strengthen its position through a Franco-German axis. So sensitive were the Americans to this 'threat' that, when France and West Germany signed in 1963 a Treaty of Friendship, President Kennedy called it 'an unfriendly act'.[7] Second, the agreement in 1957 between the six members of the ECSC to establish the EEC brought with it new discriminatory policies, such as a Customs Union with a Common External Tariff (CET) and a Common Agricultural Policy (CAP). These policies would damage US exports to Europe and elsewhere, particularly if Britain negotiated entry to the EEC with preferential deals for its Commonwealth and dependencies. Third, France exploded its first atomic bomb in 1960 and de Gaulle proceeded to develop the *force de frappe* and make much capital of the need for Western Europe as a whole to have an independent deterrent. After all, the Soviet launch of Sputnik in 1957 and the Cuban missile crisis in 1962 raised two important questions: would the US wage nuclear war for Europe? And might not the US drag Europe into a nuclear conflict that had little bearing on European interests?

The American answer to all of this was a utopian dream. Britain should enter the EEC to improve the latter's Atlanticist perspective. A multilateral nuclear force (MLNF) should be developed to give the semblance of nuclear equality among NATO's key members but establishing overall US control. And in Kennedy's Grand Design of 4 July 1962, Congress would approve the Trade Expansion Act and thus enable the US to use the next GATT talks to develop some sort of transatlantic free trade area. These ideas betrayed a gross misreading of the political environment in Europe and of the extent of American power. Neither France nor Britain was prepared to give up an independent nuclear deterrent and the MLNF was finally compromised when Kennedy, still trying to rebuild Anglo–American relations after the 1956 Suez Crisis, felt compelled to offer Prime Minister Macmillan Polaris missiles in December 1962. This deal at Nassau also provided de Gaulle with the perfect excuse to veto British membership of the EEC in 1963: Britain would be a 'Trojan Horse' for American interests in Europe and pervert the course of integration. As for US ideas of a transatlantic free trade area, these too failed to materialise. Instead, the Dillon round demonstrated that the EEC's growing power meant that the US could no longer dominate GATT and relations between the two degenerated into the first serious trade dispute in 1962, the so-called 'Chicken War'.[8]

The remainder of the 1960s saw American leadership under increasing pressure. There was fierce criticism from within NATO about US action in Vietnam. Britain, America's most trusted ally, refused to send even token forces to its aid. Even more significant was de Gaulle's continuing challenge. The importance of the US nuclear guarantee prevented West Germany from sacrificing Washington for Paris, but it could not dissuade either de Gaulle or West German Chancellor Brandt from establishing economic and cultural ties with the Eastern bloc, the latter's initiative becoming known as *Ostpolitik*. Nor could the US prevent de Gaulle from undermining its political and economic position. In 1966, he damaged NATO by withdrawing France from its military command structure and forcing the removal of both the organisation's headquarters and 26,000 US troops from French soil. In 1967, he again thwarted US hopes to use Britain to open up the EEC by vetoing its entry for a second time. Furthermore, he successfully attacked the Bretton Woods system, which was seen as the hallmark of US economic hegemony. De Gaulle speculated against sterling and in the mid-1960s demanded that the US Treasury redeem in gold several hundred million dollars. This helped force British devaluation in November 1967, set off another wave of speculation against the dollar, and ensured that by 1970 US ambitions for the Bretton Woods system and multilateralism were in free-fall.

1970–89: competitive co-operation

From 1970 through to 1989, the US made intermittent efforts to improve transatlantic relations, particularly once de Gaulle had left the political scene. For example, the Nixon administration declared 1973 the 'Year of Europe' and in 1978 Carter made the first presidential visit to the European Commission in Brussels. Also, GATT continued to be used to mitigate increasing economic friction, and offset agreements with West Germany made a limited contribution to financing the deployment of US troops there. Overall, though, the period brought little success for American hopes that Europe would either accept economic sacrifices to underwrite the American economy, or defer to Washington's political leadership, or become more outward looking. Instead, it revealed both that the balance of power had shifted markedly and that the US was increasingly out of step with Western Europe.[9]

Nixon reacted to the problems of the 1960s by trying to develop as many bilateral links as possible between Washington and West European capitals in the hope that this would give the US more leverage than dealing with the European institutions alone. Nevertheless, the US received increasingly selective support on both Cold War and economic issues because Western Europe was conscious of its growing economic power and felt little threat from the East. In the early 1970s, West Germany refused to help the dollar and, despite Nixon's attempts to prevent it, the Bretton Woods system duly collapsed. Also, most NATO members refused to support the US during the Yom Kippur War in 1973 and, in June 1980, the EC declared against US policy and in favour of a Palestinian homeland and Palestinian participation in Arab–Israeli peace talks. Furthermore, there was generally lukewarm support for Reagan's hardline stance against the Soviets. Western Europe resented Washington's simultaneous insistence on bilateral American–Soviet talks and demands that Europe should make greater commitments to containment. Major popular opposition developed to the deployment of US cruise missiles, West European states refused to abandon growing economic links with the East, and co-operation within organisations such as COCOM (a committee which oversaw the West's multilateral strategic embargo against communist states) continued to be troublesome.

Transatlantic friction was particularly acute during Reagan's first term.[10] His resurrection of the Anglo–American Special Relationship with Margaret Thatcher revived the long-debated issue of Britain's commitment to integration, even though it had finally joined the EC in 1973. Even more important was Reagan's extreme sensitivity about US leadership. As the EC enlarged and its economic strength grew, so too did the inherent tension between European political integration and reliance upon US leadership in NATO. When France proposed reactivating the WEU in 1984, which had become obscured by NATO, the Reagan administration feared that it was an implicit challenge to NATO supremacy. When the EC agreed on the 1986 Single European Act, which aimed to create a single European market by 1992, Reagan responded with protectionist measures and alarmist images of a 'Fortress Europe'. And when it came to international trade, Washington and Brussels were frequently locked in conflict. The Commission studiously avoided liberalising European policies lest it damage either European competitiveness or the fragile political consensus that was necessary for further integration. This, coupled with European introversion as economic depression hit in the early 1980s, meant that the CAP continued to be a major transatlantic sore, as did issues relating to banking, insurance, public procurement, and the airline industry.[11]

Conclusion

Despite the irritant of Berlin, the Cold War condition of Europe was quickly stabilised and American policy-makers became preoccupied instead with holding their allies in check. First, it was the containment of West Germany, then resisting the French challenge, and then holding the EC in line. The results were at best mixed. Nixon once warned the Europeans that they could not have US co-operation and participation on security issues and at the same time engage in confrontation or even hostility on the political and economic fronts. He was wrong. The European nation-states knew that they were geostrategically, politically and economically invaluable to Washington and once NATO was established they were free to reassert themselves using Marshall Aid. Thereafter, US commitment to containment policy ironically allowed the Europeans to see the Cold War as an issue secondary to their post-war adjustment to the more powerful and enduring force of economic globalisation.

US policy-makers had originally accepted that short-term economic sacrifices had to be made in return for a stable Western Europe and the prospect of large markets for US exports. However, the West Europeans reneged on this implicit deal because their importance to US strategy and growing economic power meant that they soon ceased to be suppliants for US largesse. This casts doubts about notions of US hegemony and empire in Europe, a debate that remains unresolved. For example, J.L. Gaddis talks of a voluntaristic empire, R.T. Griffiths of American hegemony theory being outdated, K. Schwabe of American decline after the EDC debacle, and A.P. Dobson has strongly challenged the whole idea of a US hegemonic relationship with Europe.[12] Also in doubt is whether or not America 'won' the battle in Europe. If the battle really was simply to contain communism, then the US succeeded. However, if policy-makers misread the dominant dynamic in European capitals, then that success needs major qualification because the Europeans used the US ruthlessly for their own ends. In particular, they freewheeled in the security domain and exploited the competitive advantage that this gave them in the economic and political spheres. When the Cold War ended, the interdependence between Western Europe and the US was as immutable as it had been in the immediate post-war years. However, the balance of power had so shifted that Washington, if ever it had been, could no longer be sure of blocking West European actions, let alone determining them. The European Community had enlarged to twelve countries[13] and further admissions were certain to follow the collapse of the Berlin Wall. Its economic power within GATT and potentially protectionist policies, such as CAP and the Single Market, threatened to run against US interests. And a combination of the end of the Cold War and strong French interest in security arrangements, which did not rely upon the US, posed serious questions about the future of NATO, and with it American influence and commitments in Europe.

6   Hegemony and the Western Hemisphere

Debate about US power is endless, but there is a consensus that it has been preponderant since 1945. Following on from this comes the claim that the US is an hegemon, which created stability by inducing others to follow rules in a system of which it was the architect. According to hegemony theory, the hegemon usually prevails over others, not by the use of force, but by socialising them into its norms. In the case of the US, this means the free market in the economic sphere, liberal politics and anti-communism in the political.[1]

Hegemonic leadership, however, involves costs, which erode power differentials. Thus, massive US economic and military aid to Western Europe and Japan allowed others to flourish in the system without them having to pay for its maintenance. The hegemon sows the seeds of its own destruction: relative decline is its unavoidable fate. This is a sophisticated recasting of the theory of the rise and decline of empires (discussed in Chapter 10): in the end over-stretch brings down the *imperium*. For the moment, however, the focus is on US relations in the Western Hemisphere, which appear to have been truly hegemonic since 1945.

After the Second World War, the US had important security interests to protect in the region, most notably the Panama Canal Zone, which the US had obtained in 1905 and which provided a short route for the US navy between the Atlantic and the Pacific. The US also had important investments, markets and sources of supply in Latin America. To post-war US leaders, all these interests were threatened by communism. As in Europe, the fear was not of a red army, but of red ideas subverting countries from within. With the global challenge from communism it seemed essential to ensure that the rules of the system – market economies, liberal political values, and anti-communism – should at least be enforced in 'the backyard'. With these containment ideas in mind, the US signed the Rio Military Pact in 1947, which promulgated the principle that an attack on any American state would be taken as an attack on them all. A year later, a further hemispheric management structure was created at Bogota, the Organisation of American States (OAS). Contrary to US wishes, Article 15 of the OAS charter outlawed intervention in the internal or external affairs of any other state. This principle was soon flouted.

Guatemala 1954

The first challenge to the hegemonic prerogatives of the US arose in Central America and set a pattern for the future. In 1944, Guatemala got rid of General Jorge Ubico, who had compared his brand of justice with God's and Hitler's. There followed a period of mild reform to deal with maldistribution of land – the most serious economic problem of Latin America. In Guatemala 50% of the population held 3% of the land and the élite 2% held 60%. In 1951, a more robust reformer came to power, Jacobo Arbentz Guzman, but he had the problem of the Boston-based United Fruit Company (UFC), which owned over 60% of the arable land, paid low wages, cheated the government out of legitimate revenue, and under-utilised the land it owned.

In March 1953, Arbenz appropriated a quarter million acres from the UFC and offered to compensate the company at the level it had valued the land for tax purposes – $600,000. The UFC responded by demanding $15.8 million: a sum that John Foster Dulles, US Secretary of State, pronounced as no less than required by international law. Unfortunately for Arbenz, both John Foster and his brother Allen Dulles, Director of the CIA, had close connections with the UFC through their family law firm.

Over the following months there followed a murky story of intrigue and propaganda. Guatemala received a shipment of small arms from the Eastern bloc and was falsely denounced as communist. John Foster Dulles conjured up the spectre of a communist assault on the Panama Canal Zone, of reds swarming up (over 1,000 miles from Guatemala) to, and then no doubt beyond, the Central American isthmus into Mexico and onto the US itself. As opposition to Arbenz was stirred up, the CIA laid its plans. They found a willing collaborator in Colonel Castillo Armas.

The CIA colluded with the long-established Somoza dictatorship in Nicaragua and trained troops there under Armas. The propaganda war was stepped up and then, on 8 June 1954, Armas led a small army into Guatemala. Its success was not immediate and so American-flown planes dropped charges of dynamite on Guatemala City, after which the government and its army parted company: Arbenz was isolated. Armas took over, returned the land to the UFC, and shot most of the supporters of the previous regime. His government was corrupt and it brutalised and held back the development of the country. This was a classic case of neo-imperialism: control without the trappings of formal empire. There were all the components identified by New Left writers such as William Appleman Williams: the economic forces of capitalism, the power of government enlisted for their defence, propaganda and subversion of the democratic process, the use of secretive and largely unaccountable power of the state in the form of the CIA, and the demonisation of the enemy as communist.[2] This pattern, with minor variations, was to occur time and again in the Western Hemisphere once the Guatemala coup had set the precedent. But, it was not just Americans who learnt from this. Fidel Castro would not make the same mistake as Guzman and allow a feeble military attack to cut away his military support. In Cuba he created a people's army that would require more than a minor surgical operation to sever it from its political leaders.

The Alliance for Progress

1958, 1959 and 1961 were symbolically important for the US. In 1958, US Vice President Richard Nixon was spat upon in Caracas. On New Year's Day 1959, Fidel Castro and his guerrilla army marched into Havana and ended the much hated, violent, oppressive and deeply corrupt regime of Fulgencio Batista. In January 1961, Nikita Krushchev, buoyed up with recent communist technological and economic successes and the upsurge of radical movements in the Third World, belligerently announced that the Soviet Union would support the rising tide of liberation movements. A gauntlet had been thrown down, this time not for a direct duel between the First and Second Worlds, but for one fought indirectly for the hearts and minds of the Third World. If this duel were to be won by the US, it had to be won first and foremost in the backyard. Here the US response was two-fold: more intervention, and $20 billion of aid over ten years through the Alliance for Progress proposed by Kennedy on 13 March 1961.

Presidents Kennedy and Johnson both aimed to foster peaceful reform and economic prosperity in Latin America, but they had only marginal success. The US was caught on the horns of a dilemma: it disapproved of oppressive right-wing regimes in the region, but preferred them to the spread of communism and so for the sake of a 'greater good' supported them in the vain hope that some day they would reform themselves. After Castro's victory the Americans had living vindication of their fears: Marxism had broken through the hemispheric perimeter. However, much of this was a self-fulfilling prophecy: in supporting oppressive regimes for fear of communism, the US made it more difficult for indigenous reform movements to progress. Non-communist opposition groups saw US aid come in and no reforms take place, so they looked elsewhere for outside help and found it in the Soviet bloc. The rebels thus came to hate the US and to associate with communism. This action-reaction syndrome nurtured conditions for the spread of the very thing that the US was trying to eliminate.

The Alliance for Progress failed. It helped to increase Latin American economic growth to about 5% *per annum* by the mid-1960s, but wealth accumulated in the élite, not the people and there was little land or tax reform. Effectively, the Alliance for Progress strengthened and enriched the forces of oppression. By 1970, there were over a dozen more military regimes in Latin America than in 1960. Cuba, despite a military invasion in 1961 and the trauma of the missile crisis in 1962, remained under Castro's control. Meanwhile, the romantic features and revolutionary adventures in Latin America of his lieutenant, Che Guevara, created an icon for dissatisfied youth throughout the world. The challenge of communism in the Western Hemisphere was still perceived as potent in Washington. If the Soviets could get one client state, they could get more and that, for economic, strategic (especially after the missile crisis), and political reasons, had to be prevented. Aid continued, but also the implacable resolve not to allow another country to go communist. That meant intervention as and when necessary.

As and when necessary

The American invasions of the Dominican Republic in 1965 and of Grenada in 1983 have similarities. In the Dominican Republic, repression by the military government of Donald Reid Cabral, who was backed by the US, caused instability. Part of the opposition was branded as communist, though it was not a particularly strong faction. In Grenada, the situation became unstable as the pro-Cuba radical Michael Bishop was assassinated in 1983 and replaced by the even more radical Bernard Coard. There were ties between Grenada, Cuba and the Soviet Union, and Cubans were busy building a large runway that the CIA alleged could be used for refuelling Soviet planes. The US had justifiable fears about threats to the Panama Canal and the strategic sea-lanes in the Gulf of Mexico. In both the Dominican Republic and Grenada cases, the US made much of the danger of communism and the threat to the lives of US citizens. It was this latter point that was used as the pretext for the respective invasions. A semblance of peace was created in the Dominican Republic, though political repression continued. In Grenada there were elections and a new, less radical, government took over.

because of its consequences in the Second World War. Kennedy felt that the US had to be resolute, send the right messages to Krushchev, and get the missiles out of Cuba. Among other things, this would prevent the Soviets from using them as a bargaining ploy to make gains elsewhere, such as in the Western redoubt in Berlin, or regarding US missile deployments in Turkey. The Americans felt that if they gave way to blackmail, then the Soviets, like all blackmailers, would be back for a second, third and fourth, *tranche*. The great danger with this was that eventually the US would have to say no, but then it would have lost credibility. The Soviets would not believe American protestations. The supposed bluff would be called and nuclear war would probably follow. These important considerations were much written about soon after the crisis. More recently, however, evidence has come to light that Kennedy's commitment to flexible response held an option in reserve that would have gone down, if not an appeasement-like, at least an accommodating route that actually involved a trade of Soviet Cuban for US missiles in Turkey.[3]

The Soviet role in the crisis also had complications, some of which have only recently been revealed. Although Kennedy felt under pressure from Soviet foreign policy and what he saw as Soviet-inspired liberation movements, Krushchev also felt threatened. Kennedy's rhetoric was combative. An invasion force had assaulted Cuba and the US had embarked upon a massive rearmament programme. Moreover, although the Soviets had taken the lead in ICBMs and boasted of their power and that they had no need to station them outside of Soviet boundaries, in fact, the programme had gone disastrously wrong. Krushchev knew that the Soviet Union in the short-term was vulnerable to a US first-strike. Placing IRBMs and MRBMs on Cuba could help to close this window of vulnerability. But, perhaps more important for Krushchev was the fear of damage to the cause of liberation movements, to which he had publicly committed himself, if Castro were to be successfully toppled by a second invasion. These two factors drove Krushchev deliberately to deceive the Americans and place missiles on Cuba.

After the Americans discovered their presence, there was never any argument about the fact that they had to go. They could not stay for three basic reasons. First, they would have had a psychological impact, which would have been very damaging politically and could have provoked a dangerous and possibly uncontrollable right-wing backlash. It was bad enough having a communist state in the Western Hemisphere. To have a nuclear capable one was just not acceptable. It would have altered the perceptions of the relative standing of the US and the Soviet Union in the Cold War and, as Kennedy commented, perceptions contribute to reality. Second, the missiles on Cuba would have strengthened the Soviet

Union's strike capability and cut down on the warning time. Third, if the Soviets had been allowed to succeed in developing a nuclear base on Cuba, it might have encouraged them to other acts of adventurism and a blundering into unintentional nuclear war.

However, consensus on the need to remove the missiles did not translate into consensus on what to do. Before telling the world about the missiles Kennedy established the Executive Committee of the NSC (EXCOM) to consider policy options. It was comprised of key personnel from the NSC, Soviet specialists, the foreign policy establishment and people close to the President, most notably his brother, Attorney General Robert Kennedy. The EXCOM's initial enthusiasm for an air strike soon receded when it became clear that it would involve Soviet casualties, that the military could not guarantee 100% success and that a follow-up invasion would very probably be needed. The EXCOM eventually produced six options: do nothing; apply diplomatic pressure; ease Castro away from the Soviets; impose a naval blockade; mount an air strike; invade. This range of options was whittled down to the idea of using limited force in the form of a blockade, or quarantine, as it was less provocatively called, with the military options held in reserve. From being hawkish at the outset, the EXCOM pulled back under pressure, particularly from the Kennedys and Defense Secretary Robert McNamara. The most dove-like official had been Adlai Stevenson, who wanted to make concessions and stick to diplomacy. For years, people thought that this had been entirely rejected by Kennedy, but recent evidence indicates otherwise.

On Monday 22 October, the President announced the discovery of the missiles and went on to make seven main points: the US would impose a naval quarantine to prevent further shipments of aggressive weapons; there would be increased surveillance and US forces would stand ready to meet all eventualities; any nuclear strike from Cuba anywhere in the Western Hemisphere would be deemed to be a direct Soviet attack upon the US; US forces at Guantanamo Bay would be strengthened; the US would co-ordinate with the OAS and NATO; a meeting of the UN Security Council would discuss the situation; and Kennedy called upon Krushchev to end this threat to peace.

Krushchev's initial response was truculent, but on Wednesday, when the quarantine came into operation, Soviet ships turned back. On Friday, the Americans showed their resolve without being over-provocative by stopping and boarding a US built, Greek-crewed, Lebanese-registered ship chartered by the Soviets. The same day they received an offer from Krushchev: he would remove the missiles in return for a guarantee of Cuba's sovereignty. But then, on the following day, the Soviets publicly demanded that the US remove its nuclear missiles from Turkey.

Kennedy went along with the view of the majority in EXCOM that there could be no public trade of missiles because it would have undermined allied faith in the US. Nevertheless, Kennedy mused at one point that it would not look good in the history books if there were a nuclear war because he had refused to withdraw obsolete weapons. The Americans decided to accept the first offer from Krushchev and ignore the second one. At the same time, Robert Kennedy arranged a meeting with Soviet Ambassador Dobrynin. He explained the political difficulties for the US that a public connection between the removal of Cuban and Turkish missiles would cause, but he undertook to remove them unilaterally within a short period of time. This decision was not taken in the EXCOM. Neither was another important decision made by John Kennedy. He instructed Secretary of State, Dean Rusk, to prime an ex-American UN official, Andrew Cordier. In the event of the quarantine not working and the situation deteriorating, Cordier should stand by to approach UN Secretary General U-Thant and ask him, as an independent third party, to propose a trade of the Turkish for the Cuban missiles. Whether Kennedy would have taken this more accommodating path, or, whether he would have resorted to military action, we shall never know. On 28 October Krushchev agreed to remove the missiles in return for a US guarantee to respect Cuban sovereignty.

The crisis was at an end, but it had been a close run thing. Many came to see it as a model for successful crisis management, but not everything was under such tight control as one might have wished. A US U-2 high altitude reconnaissance plane strayed perilously into Soviet air space during the crisis and one was shot down by Cuban and Soviet gunfire on Saturday 27 October. The Americans badly miscalculated the size of the Soviet force on Cuba and, unknown to them, if they had invaded they would have been confronted by Soviet troops equipped with battlefield atomic weapons. Orders issued by the President and his immediate lieutenants were not always carried out and control over the Soviet nuclear arsenal on Cuba depended upon the loyalty of the local commander.[4]

What did the US learn from the crisis and what came after? Both the US and the Soviet Union were deeply disturbed by the crisis and several developments followed rapidly in its wake. A hot-line between the White House and the Kremlin was installed. Emphasis was placed on stabilising the superpower nuclear relationship and progress was forthcoming from arms talks. In 1963, the Partial Test Ban Treaty was signed and, despite Vietnam, the two superpowers gradually moved towards *détente* and SALT.

US relations with Cuba remained hostile. The economic embargo still continues and was given added bite by the Helms-Burton Act in 1995.

Periodically, problems have flared up over refugees and Soviet military activities. In 1979 the 'discovery' of a Soviet brigade on Cuba was made much of in the media and caused a veritable political storm until the Soviet invasion of Afghanistan stole the limelight. The issue finally faded away once it was revealed that the Kennedy administration had in fact sanctioned such troop levels on Cuba. For America, Cuba continued to be symbolically important as an outpost of communism and as a breeding ground for subversion in the Western Hemisphere. Its allies thought that this was much exaggerated while the Cold War was still being waged: why, after its end, America should continue with such hostility, they find even more difficult to understand. Perhaps this is a case where realist, objective assessments of US interests and Cuba's power to threaten them might relieve the US of considerable embarrassment: if Pope John Paul can bring himself to visit Cuba and consort with Castro, then perhaps Clinton or whoever succeeds him should as well.

Hegemony: a tentative conclusion

The US has not just been motivated by a drive to sustain its hegemonic dominance in the Western Hemisphere by cleansing it of communism and following the pattern of interventionism established by the successful coup in Guatemala. During the early Carter administration, promoting human rights, even at a temporary cost to US influence in some states, was an important feature of policy. In 1978, despite fearsome opposition, the President pushed the Panama Treaties through the Senate: they gradually ceded the Canal and the Zone back to Panama. From one perspective this was a highly moral self-denying ordinance, from another a realistic adjustment to changing political and strategic realities: both seem somewhat at odds with the idea of hegemonic leadership. In 1982, the Reagan administration was unable to bring Argentina to heel and provoked considerable opposition in Latin America by siding with Britain and against the anti-communist military junta in Buenos Aires in the Falklands War.

Even when the US pursued policies specifically designed to maintain its hemispheric leadership, it did not always prevail. Economic influence and socialisation into US norms failed in Guatemala, Cuba, the Dominican Republic, Chile, Grenada and Nicaragua. Instead, the US had to resort to covert or outright military intervention. Moreover, even when force was deployed, it was not always successful, as Cuba still amply demonstrates. Thus, hegemony is a notion that needs to be used carefully. In the US experience in the Western Hemisphere, it would appear that in the pursuit of hegemonic control, the means came to undermine the very values and institutions that hegemonic leadership was intended to preserve for the system.

7 The US and Asia, 1945–89

Asia is where the arrogance of power began and ended. In August 1945, President Truman authorised a form of indiscriminate bombing which slaughtered 400,000 Japanese civilians in Hiroshima and Nagasaki. The world awakened to the new atomic order and at its head was the US, economic powerhouse and sole possessor of the atom bomb. Thirty years later, President Nixon oversaw the conclusion of the most humbling defeat in modern American history as a Third World state forced the self-proclaimed champion of the Free World to sue for peace. The lives of 55,000 servicemen, $150 billion and 10 million tons of bombs had been squandered in a futile attempt to win a limited war in Vietnam that, for the North Vietnamese, could have no limits. Massive US military strength was insufficient to win this type of conflict, and the impact of the war on America, commonly referred to as the Vietnam syndrome, was of greater significance for its foreign and domestic policy than any other Cold War experience. An anti-war movement swept through American society and sparked a period of congressional re-assertion that challenged the imperial Presidency and hampered American leadership of the Western alliance until the Reagan revival in the 1980s.

Close behind Vietnam in significance were the questions asked of US policy-makers by China, Korea, and Japan. The loss of China in 1949 revolutionised the geostrategic topography of the Cold War and sent shockwaves that undermined the Truman administration and reverberated around American society in the form of the McCarthy witch-hunts. It also prompted one of the most bizarre episodes in US history as successive administrations refused to recognise the PRC and insisted instead that nationalists, driven onto the island of Taiwan, represented the true and only China. Then there was the Korean War.[1] This gave the stamp of legitimacy to NSC-68's globalisation of containment and defined the contours of American foreign policy for the next twenty years. Finally, there was Japan, perhaps the bitterest American enemy cheque to use military force against the PRC, including tactical nuclear weapons. It took over twenty years for the Americans to realise the error of this approach. In the meantime, they unloaded upon the rest of Asia their collective anguish at the loss of China.

Korea and growing problems in Indo-China

Hard on the heels of the loss of both China and the US atomic monopoly came Korea and Indo-China. The Korean War, among other things, enabled the Truman administration to get NSC-68 passed by a Congress hitherto unenthusiastic about increasing US commitments overseas. It was also a conflict that had been waiting to happen. During the war, America and the Soviet Union decided that, after Korea had been liberated from the Japanese, it should be temporarily divided between them during a transition phase to full independence. However, with the Soviets north and the Americans south of the 38th parallel, the onset of the Cold War portended grave possibilities. Both sides withdrew their troops but began to build up their clients. The Soviets sent military aid and advisers to develop North Korean forces, led by Kim Il Sung. The Americans, with some reservations, propped up Syngman Rhee in South Korea. He was an unpopular, petty dictator, who made only minimal genuflection to democratic principles and was an embarrassment to the US. Nevertheless, when North Korea launched a surprise attack on 25 June 1950, the US rushed to his aid, despite the fact that in January 1950, Acheson had explicitly excluded Taiwan and Korea from the US defence perimeter in Asia.

Opinion has divided about the reasons for Kim Il Sung's action. Was he Stalin's puppet or an ardent Korean nationalist? Did Rhee provoke him in the hope that war would bring Western salvation for his crumbling regime? Or was, as recent evidence suggests, Kim Il Sung given the green light by Stalin?[3] Even more important, why did the US react with such speed and force? It has been suggested that the Americans feared that a communist-controlled South Korea might incline Japan to neutralism, which would deprive them of their strongest position in Asia and their closest air bases to eastern Russia. Also, if Japan were to be developed as a counterweight to China, it needed markets and raw materials in Asia.

US troops had occupied Japan since September 1945. General MacArthur, the Supreme Allied Commander, had overseen an Americanisation of the Japanese political system which included a strong emphasis on the free market, representative government, civil liberties and decentralised power. Once the Cold War began, the US looked to a liberated Japan as a key partner and, from the 1949 Dodge mission onwards, it encouraged Japan's economic recovery. When the Korean War broke out, Truman expedited a peace treaty with Japan. Signed in September 1951, the San Francisco agreement saw the Americans successfully exclude Russian participation. They also traded reparation claims against Japan from a host of countries in return for the Japanese alliance against communism and the grant of American military bases in Japanese territory, most notably on Okinawa. Rather like the German solution in Europe, the Americans encouraged Japanese rearmament and industrialisation to create a zone of stability for the Western world. Although the Japanese never rearmed to the extent that the US desired, the US had secured the Asian ally it desperately needed. In 1956, Japan joined the UN and by 1965 its economic miracle had produced the first of its many international balance of payments surpluses.

However, important though Japan was, it is unlikely that it was the fear of a communist South Korea inspiring Japanese neutrality that triggered the US conduct of the Korean War. A much more compelling explanation is that Korea was the war that Truman needed to calm domestic critics, demonstrate US resolve in the face of communist aggression, and to forge ahead with his globalisation of containment. Korea seemed so opportune from this perspective that some scholars have suggested that US diplomacy invited the North Korean attack.[4] This is a matter of debate, but it is certain that, with Mao preparing to move once more against Chiang, McCarthyism in full spate and an uncooperative Congress concerned about defence expenditure, Truman desperately needed to sell NSC-68 to America. North Korean aggression gave him that opportunity. Furthermore, the Korean conflict was used to push through the re-militarisation of West Germany and a build-up of US forces in Europe. Kim Il Sung was portrayed as Stalin's crony and Mao's simultaneous build-up against Taiwan seemingly confirmed US assumptions about both the Sino-Soviet alliance and the monolithic nature of communism.

Capitalising upon the Soviet boycott of the Security Council, on account of the US refusal to allow the PRC to take the China seat at the UN, Truman secured the moral high ground by obtaining a 9–0 condemnation of the North Korean offensive. US countermeasures were put swiftly into place. On 26 June 1950, the Truman Doctrine was formally extended to Asia, the seventh fleet was used subsequently as an interdiction force to counter Mao's challenge to Taiwan, and military aid was extended to the French, who had engaged Ho Chi Minh's communists in Indo-China.

As for the Korean conflict itself, much was risked for little direct reward. The US committed its own troops to save Rhee as his corrupt and deeply unpopular regime failed to stem the North Korean onslaught. Under the lead of General MacArthur, United Nations troops, predominantly American and South Korean, outmanoeuvred the communists with the Inchon amphibious landings and drove the communists back. Then, instead of stopping at the declared objective of restoring the 38th parallel, Truman authorised the military liberation of Korea. This was a high-risk strategy based on the calculation that neither Russia nor China would intervene. The Americans were wrong. After the US ignored repeated Chinese warnings communicated via India, on 25 October China dispatched thousands of 'volunteers', in effect fully equipped regular troops, to repel MacArthur's push towards its border. It was a highly effective Chinese campaign and, with their point made, they withdrew and agreed to attend a UN meeting to resolve the crisis.

However, General MacArthur launched a counter offensive timed specifically to coincide with the Chinese mission to the UN. China and America's European allies were enraged. More importantly, Chinese forces intervened once more and drove MacArthur back far beyond the 38th parallel. Only after alarming bluster about atomic weapons, which sent Britain's Prime Minister Attlee scurrying to Washington to urge moderation, did MacArthur return in March 1951 to where he had started – the 38th parallel. Then, when he crossed it once more, Truman hastened to dismiss him. General Ridgway, MacArthur's successor, subsequently held the line for over two further years of fighting, including the legendary battles of Heartbreak Ridge and Pork Chop Hill, whilst the politicians wrangled over terms for an expedient peace. Truman had all that he wanted, other than the objectives articulated by the unrealistic 'roll-back' rhetoric of NSC-68. He had put to rest Western fears of appeasement, held the line in Asia, and won over Congress for a policy of global containment. In July 1953, his successor, Eisenhower, finally concluded a peace settlement that brought the war to an end with the boundaries between North and South Korea little different to those before it had started.

Vietnam – the arrogance of power challenged

As Korea wound down so another, even more important, issue in Asia began to gather momentum. When the French, with US support, reoccupied Vietnam after the war, the Viet Minh went into active resistance. Ho Chi Minh, their leader, was an ardent nationalist and told the US of his desire for Vietnamese independence, democracy and land reform. The Cold War prevented a sympathetic American response. There was too great a risk that Ho Chi Minh was influenced overly by communism and, in any case, French support was much more important to Cold War containment. Thus, the US gave France financial and military aid. By 1954, it covered all French costs in Vietnam, which amounted to almost $800 million. This was still insufficient, however, either to secure the French position in Vietnam or to buy its approval of the European Defence Community (see Chapter 5).

In 1954, the Viet Minh commander, General Giap, defeated French forces at Dien Bien Phu and broke the French will to continue. The subsequent Geneva Accords partitioned Vietnam along the 17th parallel between communist and Western elements. Laos and Cambodia were to be neutral and Vietnam's fate was to be determined by a national election in 1956. The American problem was that Ho Chi Minh was liable to secure up to 80% of the vote. Consequently, the US not only refused to sign the Geneva Accords but also flouted them by giving military support to the leader of South Vietnam, Ngo Dinh Diem. Furthermore, the US turned a blind eye to his persecution of opposition elements and sanctioned his indefinite postponement of elections. By 1958, the US looked set for a long-haul Cold War campaign. It championed an unpopular dictator against both national aspirations and the will of the international community. It also paid most of Diem's military costs, heavily subsidised his economy, and stood in clear contravention of Geneva as it established a US Military Mission of over a thousand men in South Vietnam. Yet Diem still seemed to be losing, and the US faced a difficult choice of what to do next.

When J.F. Kennedy inherited Vietnam from Eisenhower, the US commitment was still relatively small and limited strictly to economic and technical assistance. There was every possibility that Kennedy could have used the change of presidency to pull the US out of Vietnam in much the same way that Eisenhower had done in Korea. Indeed, his two most experienced European allies, Harold Macmillan and Charles de Gaulle, both warned against becoming sucked deeper into Vietnam. However, Kennedy ignored their advice. As the first Democrat president after Truman, he was vulnerable to charges of being soft on communism and, as far as he was concerned, Vietnam was pivotal to the interests of the free world in South East Asia. It had little intrinsic value but was vitally important in the interrelated context of the domino theory and of US assumptions about its vested interest in the world economic system. If communism triumphed in Vietnam, then Burma, Thailand, India, Japan, the Philippines, Cambodia and Laos would all be threatened. This would devastate the interests of the free world because it needed Asian markets and friendship, especially Japan's, where, from the 1949 Dodge Plan onwards, the US had assumed that reindustrialisation would work only if it had suitable markets and access to cheap raw materials in the Asian rimlands. Moreover, the US faced a series of adverse international events, notably the 1956 Suez Crisis and the failed Hungarian uprising that year, the Soviet launch of Sputnik in 1957, the weakened state of the US economy, and the double setbacks in 1961 of the failed intervention in Cuba and the building of the Berlin Wall. US credibility seemed in question. This was particularly acute when it came to showing resolve in the fight against communism in non-Western countries because, as an East–West nuclear balance began to emerge, there were much greater restrictions on vigorous action directly between the superpowers. In short, the ideological blinkers of containment, domestic political considerations and adverse international events all combined to lead Kennedy onto a tragic misjudgement. He assumed that US credibility depended upon victory in Vietnam and mortgaged it accordingly.

Kennedy was keen to develop a flexible response initiative both to wage containment in the Third World, which was the new focus of American efforts, and to mitigate the problems created by Eisenhower's big bomb approach. In particular, he looked to combine nation-building with economic aid and the development of a counterinsurgency force, the Green Berets, to combat guerrilla warfare. Vietnam was Kennedy's testing ground. For two years, Kennedy persisted with Eisenhower's choice of puppet in Saigon, Diem, and supplied the South Vietnamese Army (ARVN) with increasing amounts of military hardware and US advisers: 15,000 by 1963. However, as Diem's unpopularity grew, he became worse than an embarrassment to the US, and in November 1963 the CIA successfully encouraged ARVN generals to lead a military coup. Diem was murdered and the Americanisation of the Vietnam War had begun.

Ironically, Kennedy did not live to see the full consequences of his actions. Less than a month later, he was also assassinated and it fell to Lyndon Johnson to deal with a strengthened US commitment to, and a badly deteriorating situation in, Vietnam. In many ways, Johnson was trapped by the actions of his predecessor and by an American political system that was not yet ready to abandon either the rigidities of anti-communism or the fallacies of the arrogance of power. What Johnson did was logical and almost universally supported: he escalated the conflict. In July 1964, UN Secretary General U Thant joined Moscow, Hanoi and Paris in calling for the US to attend an international conference in Geneva to discuss Vietnam. Johnson refused and underlined American determination to stay in Vietnam by announcing a 30% increase in US military advisers to South Vietnam. The following month, Johnson used a minor skirmish between US warships and North Vietnamese PT-boats to push through Congress the infamous Gulf of Tonkin Resolution. By a vote of 416 to 0 in the House of Representatives and 88 to 2 in the Senate, Congress surrendered abjectly its constitutional duty to restrain the Executive and bestowed upon Johnson a blank cheque to wage war upon Asia. In February 1965, he launched an intensive bombing campaign against North Vietnam, Operation Rolling Thunder, and when it became clear that the Air Force could not, after all, bomb Hanoi into submission, escalated the land battle dramatically. On 28 July 1965, he approved sending 100,000 US ground troops to Vietnam and by 1968 the US had committed half a million men to fight for a tiny country of no intrinsic strategic value.

Johnson withdrew from the 1968 presidential race amid growing domestic turmoil as the anti-war movement became stronger, the Cold War consensus began to disintegrate, and the US economy faltered. Worst of all, the Tet Offensive, which won the communists spectacular if short-lived physical gains, brought Hanoi a psychological triumph that destroyed the American will to win. His successor, the Republican Richard Nixon, was elected to extricate the US from Vietnam with honour. It was an unenviable task. The US public would not tolerate much more carnage. A $20 billion gap in its balance of payments meant that the US economy imposed further limits on policy options, and a guilt-ridden Congress was looking to redeem its credentials by transferring blame for Vietnam to the Executive.

Nixon and his NSA, Henry Kissinger, set about a carefully crafted strategy to deny North Vietnam foreign support, gradually reduce American commitment to the South, and build a position from which to negotiate a peace. The isolation of North Vietnam from its allies was pursued through developing *détente* with the Soviets and opening relations with the PRC. To liberate room for manoeuvre, Nixon abandoned the draft at home and introduced Vietnamisation abroad, which effectively substituted South Vietnamese for politically sensitive American troops. On 8 June 1968, Nixon announced the first withdrawal of 25,000 troops and by 1972 US forces were down to 70,000. Over the same period South Vietnamese forces rose from 700,000 to over a million. With the sting taken out of the protest movements, Nixon moved simultaneously to create the illusion of American ascendancy in Vietnam whilst engaging Hanoi in peace negotiations in Paris. In April 1970, Nixon announced that US forces had invaded Cambodia to cut off communist supply lines, and for similar reasons the US provided air cover for an ARVN invasion of Laos in February 1971. However, the Cambodian invasion was an illegal act that provoked Congress to reassert itself. On 31 December 1970, it repealed the Gulf of Tonkin resolution and, when Nixon ignored this, stated specifically that no future monies appropriated for military expenditure could be used to widen the war. In 1973, Congress also passed the War Powers Act.

However, all of this was too late either to deter Nixon or redeem US credibility. On 23 January 1973, Nixon claimed peace with honour as a cease-fire ended all US participation in the war. This was undoubtedly the best that Nixon could have hoped for in the circumstances. The fact remained, though, that despite dropping more bombs on Vietnam than Johnson and making the ARNV technically the fourth ranking military power in the world by 1975, Nixon oversaw the first war that the US had lost in modern history. The peace treaty was not worth the paper it was written on and Thieu, the ultimate US choice to head South Vietnam after Ky and Diem, was quickly embroiled in conflict once more. Congress refused President Ford's request for money to help him. In April 1975, Thieu fled the country, South Vietnam surrendered unconditionally on 30 April, and Saigon was renamed Ho Chi Minh City.[5]

Post-Vietnam US policy in Asia: trusted ally and the strategic triangle

In July 1971, Nixon revealed new US thinking that had in part emerged from the debacle of Vietnam. In future, calculations of power had to be much more sophisticated and based primarily upon economics, because this was the key to all other forms of power. He and Kissinger also saw an advantageous systemic shift from a bipolar to a multipolar configuration of power that would reduce dangerous rigidities and facilitate greater opportunities for developing a shared concept of a world order. Although there were many *loci* of power, five were overwhelmingly important – America, the Soviet Union, Western Europe, China and Japan. Asia thus remained the primary focus of US foreign policy, even after Vietnam.

In January 1973, Kissinger embraced trilateralism, which identified the US, Western Europe and Japan as the powerhouses of liberal capitalism. Japan was now a key centre of world power and had to be given the same attention as Western Europe. Although the US had presided over the birth of the new Japan, this was a relationship in need of work because it did not automatically follow that the Japanese would tow the American line. Indeed, neither Nixon nor Kissinger had good relations with the Japanese. In 1971 they inadvertently upset them, first by not telling them of a proposed visit by Kissinger to Peking in July and then by imposing both an import surcharge and a temporary ban on converting dollars into gold. In the aftermath of the 1973 oil crisis, Japan pursued a policy in contradiction of the American line. And Carter had little success in securing Japanese co-operation when in 1978–79 the US annual trade deficit totalled some $40 billion, of which $12 billion was derived from the Japanese trade surplus. Corrective measures were imperative and required Japan to help more in managing the global economy and to relieve some US expenditure overseas by increasing its security spending. On both counts the Japanese refused.

Nevertheless, the US managed to retain Japan as a vital geostrategic ally and an increasingly important trading partner. In 1972, Okinawa reverted to Japanese sovereignty, but it was agreed that the enormous US base there should remain. Likewise, the Japanese avoided confrontation with the US when the latter drove down the value of the dollar which resulted in the 1986–88 'high yen shock'. Furthermore, in the 1980s Japan agreed with the US about its 'third opening to the world'. This was symbolised by the Structural Impediments Initiative which was designed to make Japanese markets more accessible to American goods in order to redress their trade imbalance. All things considered Japan remained a trustworthy ally throughout the Cold War, even if its growing economic power potentially rivalled that of the US.[6]

In stark contrast to the robust US friendship with Japan was its fragile relationship with China. Mao's alliance with the Soviet Union in 1950 had been reluctant and by 1960 it was over. The Soviets withdrew all technical and economic advisers, refused to give Mao a nuclear capability, and withheld support in the 1962 India–China border skirmish. China denounced the USSR after Khrushchev's unilateral revision of communist orthodoxy in 1956 and laid claim thereafter to ideological pre-eminence in the socialist world. In 1958, China embarked upon the Great Leap Forward, a new economic policy to try to harness its greatest natural resource – people power – and, by 1966, Mao had become embroiled in both the Cultural Revolution and a bitter border dispute with the Soviets. All of this, coupled with Chinese moderation concerning Vietnam, finally revealed the error of the 1949 US judgement about communism being a monolithic monster to be slain wherever it raised its head. New opportunities were at hand and Nixon, faced with a reassertive Congress, serious questions about US leadership of the global economy, and a no-win position in Vietnam, needed desperately to capitalise upon them.

Between 1969 and 1972, thirty-two countries recognised the PRC and in 1971 it was finally admitted to both the UN and its Security Council. There was no point resisting the inevitable and, even though it represented one of the most startling U-turns in the history of US foreign policy, Nixon jumped aboard the Chinese bandwagon. In February 1972, he made an historic visit to China. Diplomatic contact was established, both countries renounced hegemonic ambitions in East Asia and an agreement was reached to defer the divisive issue of Taiwan. Nixon's principal objective was to give the US sufficient leverage amid the Sino-

Soviet schism to force both to abandon support of North Vietnam and allow the US to extricate itself with what credibility it had left intact. There is little evidence to suggest that this 'strategic triangle' worked. Hanoi was never controlled by either China or Russia and the outside support it received was negligible compared to that which the US gave to South Vietnam. Nevertheless, Nixon's legacy was a new era of Sino-American relations, which was formalised in January 1979 by President Carter when he opened formal diplomatic relations.

After normalisation, relations developed at an unprecedented pace. In contrast, US–Soviet relations underwent a significant downturn when the Soviet Union invaded Afghanistan in 1979, and this decline continued once Reagan reinvigorated fears about Soviet military power. Consequently, strategic considerations became paramount in America's China policy. An agreement was struck to share intelligence information on the Soviet Union and Carter's Secretary of Defense, Harold Brown, made successful overtures about defence co-operation. In September 1980, twenty licences were granted for US exports of military support equipment, a blind eye was turned toward Chinese engagement of Vietnamese forces in Cambodia, and in 1985 the Peace Pearl programme was initiated to upgrade China's new F-8 II interceptor. Once China had been granted MFN trading status, significant economic and cultural exchanges also began to take place. In addition, both the Carter and Reagan administrations were keen to co-operate with China on arms sales, drug enforcement, environmental protection, and nuclear non-proliferation.

However, not everything in the 1980s augured well for future Sino-American relations. The Reagan administration sought to destroy the nuclear balance by announcing the SDI initiative, appropriating funds for the MX ICBM and the B-1 bomber, and obtaining the agreement of key Western allies to deploy Pershing II missiles. This downgraded the importance of the strategic triangle and, coupled with Reagan's Sinophobia, led the US to take greater risks with Sino-US relations. For example, in 1982 Reagan sparked a major diplomatic row when he sold F-15 E/F aircraft to Taiwan. Although China was somewhat mollified in August, when America agreed gradually to reduce such arms sales in return for Chinese acceptance of a peaceful settlement of the PRC-Taiwan relationship, the issue was not resolved and simply transferred to the backburner. The Reagan administration also kept a very close check on both US liberalisation of technology transfers to China and the activities of COCOM members. Furthermore, the fact remained that China was a communist country with a culture and principles that the US found difficult to condone without compromising its self-pronounced moral superiority and its own doctrines. At times this led to provocative US behaviour such as in 1985 when Congress terminated funding to a UN agency that supported China's family planning programme.[7]

Conclusion

Asia witnessed the arrival of the American arrogance of power and subsequently dispatched it with devastating repercussions for US foreign policy and American society. Korea was as much, if not more, about Truman's battle at home and with his Western allies as it was with communism. America's intervention was initially unilateral and without prior consultation with its allies. The fig leaf of legitimacy accorded their action by the US-dominated UN Security Council scarcely disguised American ambitions: Korea was a war both to justify and signal the arrival of global containment. It justified the consolidation of the US position in Japan, the role of the seventh fleet as Chiang's lifeline against Mao, and the rearming of West Germany against the wishes of key US allies. It helped to formalise US primacy in the Pacific when the ANZUS security pact was signed in 1951 with Australia and New Zealand. It also brought about congressional approval of the remilitarisation that was required if NATO were to have sufficient muscle to back its objectives.

Korea also sold NSC-68 to America and secured for the presidency awesome powers. Selective service was reintroduced, a $50 billion defence budget was waved through Congress, six divisions were dispatched to Europe, massive expansion of the armed forces took place, new bases were secured in countries such as fascist Spain, and talks began to allow Greece and Turkey into NATO. Moreover, patterns in American society and in its economy were changed radically. Global containment gave a tremendous fillip to the economy through the development of an enormous industrial-military complex and, coupled with McCarthyism, helped to perpetuate the neglect of many domestic problems, such as poverty and institutionalised racial discrimination. Furthermore, Korea heralded the arrival of the imperial presidency. Truman waged war without the sanction of Congress and accumulated massive powers in the hands of the Executive.

For the next twenty years the American constitutional system was undermined as the imperial presidency prosecuted global containment. That ended when Asia, in the form of Vietnam, restored the balance. American intervention in Vietnam was consistent with containment and the escalation of the conflict was frighteningly logical. American failure provoked an 'agonising reappraisal' of a sort very different to that with which Dulles threatened Europe during the EDC negotiations. The humbling of the world's greatest superpower by a tiny, backward, Asian country cost America its unquestioned leadership of the Atlantic alliance and lent succour to new Third World challenges to the West. It also cost it the loss of bipartisan foreign policy, the imperial presidency, and the decline of unconditional support among the American people for containment.

The Vietnam War Memorial stands in Washington D.C. as an austere, but unspeakably moving, tribute to those who died for their country. They did not win in the jungles of Asia, but they bequeathed important lessons that marked a watershed in the Cold War. Congress, with the added spur of Watergate, was provoked into doing what it was supposed to do, check the Executive. Vietnam also brought home to the American people the hypocrisy of US foreign policy. What sort of society could justify a military campaign, in a distant and insignificant country, which involved such indiscriminate and ultimately rather pointless violence? Finally, Vietnam demanded a rethinking of the blinding simplicity of containment and of calculations of power based predominantly on military might. As neither China nor Russia controlled Vietnamese communism, the war exploded myths about monolithic communism and wreaked havoc upon assumptions that vital US interests were at stake everywhere. Likewise, newfound vulnerability, particularly when Japan and Europe prospered whilst fears developed about US overstretch and relative economic decline, challenged assumptions about the global economic system.

After Vietnam, the US approach to Asia was markedly more circumspect, be it during *détente* or Reagan's re-invention of the Cold War. Containment remained the guiding principle, but it was far more nuanced as the US assessed its priorities, tactics and responses more carefully. Communism was engaged, first in the strategic triangle and later on a bilateral basis with China. Economics became the overriding concern and relations with Japan became ever more important, particularly as the US continued its relative decline. Yet, even this modified approach had only limited success and, as the Cold War ended, the US faced both old and new problems in Asia. Japan continued to security free-ride at American expense whilst its economic miracle ensured trading surpluses with the US. In addition, the reversion of Okinawa to Japanese sovereignty did not remove it as a difficult issue in American–Japanese relations. As for US–China policy, this remained even more delicate. The Taiwan Relations Act (TRA) of 1979 was an unsatisfactory compromise between China hawks and doves, and the clause that allowed continued arms sales to Taiwan had potential to flare up in the future.[8] Moreover, China remained communist and resolved upon domestic policies that the US found difficult to condone. Indeed, as the decade closed, the Chinese government sent troops into Tiananmen Square where they massacred pro-democracy dissidents and embarked subsequently on a period of repression. The 1990s promised little respite for US Asian strategists, even without Cold War considerations.

8   The US, Africa and the
Middle East, 1945–89

There could be no greater contrast between the treatment of two regions than that accorded by the US to Africa and the Middle East. US policy in the former is noteworthy not least for its neglect, except for South Africa. For much of this period it was left to America's West European allies to handle Africa. Besides, the Soviets did not mount a serious challenge there until the 1970s. In contrast, the Middle East was a theatre of fierce rivalry and high stakes. Policy struggled both to keep pace with American economic expansionism and to cope successively with containment, fears of over-extension and for oil supplies, discordant allies, decolonisation, nationalism, Zionism, and Islamic fundamentalism. It was the region in which the limits of both cohesion within the Western alliance and of US power were most evident. Furthermore, the boundaries between the two blocs were most insecure here and occasioned seven of the twenty US nuclear alerts during the Cold War.

There were, however, some similarities between Africa and the Middle East. The US was often found wanting in terms of power in both theatres and faced difficulties in dealing with different belief systems and stages of economic development. Also, these regions were both dominated by non-Cold War issues: race in Africa and religion in the Middle East. How successful were US policy-makers in dealing with the regions' problems? What was the guiding light of their policies? How did they try to project adequate power to both regions? And what lasting effects did their policies have?

The US and Africa, 1945–89

US African policy in the 1950s and 1960s was one of benign neglect of Black Africa and generally cautious support for South Africa's white apartheid regime. Unlike in more geostrategically important areas of the world, there was little correlation between success and strategies of either the USSR or of America. During this period, the Soviets capitalised upon the decolonisation process to win influence in a series of states, such as Ghana, Guinea, Mali, the Sudan and Somalia. That this influence often proved ephemeral, and that by the early 1970s former allies such as Mali and Ghana were reorienting toward the West, was due less to US action than to the internal dynamics of a fragmented continent struggling to adjust to a post-colonial world. Truman, preoccupied with Korea, neglected African affairs, as did Dulles, whose disdain for non-aligned movements did nothing for US popularity in Africa. The short-lived Kennedy era saw a more caring tone in US pronouncements on the plight of Black Africa and some gestures consistent with US liberal ideals. In 1961, for example, the US supported a UN vote that advocated an end to Portuguese rule in Angola. Similarly, when riots persuaded Belgium to reverse course on its withdrawal from the mineral rich Congo, the US supported a UN Security Council motion censuring Belgian imperialism. Subsequently, it successfully countered a Soviet candidate in the ensuing power struggle by championing the African nationalist, Cyrille Adoula, who became head of the newly independent state in 1961. Nevertheless, once Kennedy was dead and Johnson became obsessed with Vietnam, Africa largely disappeared from US concerns.

Not until the mid-1970s did Africa appear again as a significant item on the US foreign policy agenda. It was no coincidence that it was in this decade of domestic US trauma that the Soviets sought to expand their influence in Africa. Two incidents stand out: Angola and Somalia. In 1974–75, Portugal pulled out quickly from its former colony Angola, leaving behind a bitter power feud between three factions: the National Union for the Total Independence of Angola (UNITA), the National Liberation Front of Angola (FNLA), and the Popular Movement for the Liberation of Angola (MPLA). This was a civil war that the superpowers could neither leave alone nor be sufficiently concerned about to take drastic action. The Soviets supported the MPLA and, when 250 Cuban military advisers arrived to help it, South Africa sent 2000 troops to aid UNITA and the US backed both UNITA and the FNLA. Cuba responded by sending a further 14,000 troops. Eventually, a nervous post-Vietnam Congress pulled the plug on aid to the FNLA and UNITA in 1976, and the US had to accept a 'defeat'. Matters were only partially redeemed in 1977 when America provided Zaire with a combination of arms and help sufficient to repel an attack by opponents of the Seko regime, who were harboured by communist Angola.

The second major issue, which concerned Ethiopia and Somalia in the Horn of Africa, contained a bitter irony. In 1953, the US began supplying arms to Ethiopia and, in 1963, the Soviets reciprocated with Somalia. However, when Somalia occupied the Ogaden territory of Ethiopia in

1978, the superpowers switched proxies. The USSR decided to back Ethiopia and the US supplied arms to Somalia as a counterweight, thus uncomfortably supporting the aggressor. Matters became tense when 10,000 Cuban volunteers arrived to aid Ethiopia. This, coupled with South Yemen's friendship with the USSR, raised the spectre of Soviet manoeuvring to strengthen their position in the Red Sea, through which oil flowed from the Middle East. However, Carter responded decisively by reducing military aid to Somalia. This implicitly sanctioned another 'loss' to the West, but it also forced Somalia to abandon its aggression and prevented an escalation of the conflict.

Reagan was less compromising than Ford and Carter. His reinvigoration of the Cold War caused him, perhaps more than any other Cold War US president, to see Africa in colours of red versus the star-spangled banner rather than the more widely perceived black versus white. This led him to provide Somalia with substantial aid when it again locked horns with Mengistu's marxist Ethiopia in 1982. More importantly, it also led Reagan to adopt a policy of 'constructive engagement' toward South Africa, which saw the US retreat significantly from the strong support Carter had given to 'black nationalism', majority rule, and independence for Namibia from South Africa. To the discomfort of some within the Reagan administration, his policy linked the US with the white supremacist regime in Pretoria. Nevertheless, he controversially resumed military aid to UNITA and tied support for Namibian independence to Cuban withdrawal from Angola, accords for which were agreed in 1988 between South Africa, Cuba, and Namibia. In February 1984, Reagan again used the Pretoria government to reduce Soviet influence, this time by sponsoring security accords between South Africa, Angola and Mozambique. Indeed, even after American public opinion forced him to impose punitive sanctions on South Africa in March 1985, Reagan maintained his *de facto* support of Pretoria and extensive contact continued between the CIA and South African military intelligence.[1]

Perhaps even more interesting than the specifics of US Cold War policy toward Africa were the patterns and the benign neglect that it demonstrated. Republican administrations were generally much more overtly tolerant of white supremacy in South Africa than Democrats. Eisenhower largely ignored it, Nixon, in the December 1969 National Security Study Memorandum 39, famously accepted it as a fact of life unlikely to change, and Reagan dealt extensively with the Pretoria regime, regardless of domestic and international criticism. However, not even Democrats could reconcile US idealism with their foreign policy practice. During the Second World War, Roosevelt argued that, under point three of the Atlantic Charter, the peoples of the African colonies were entitled to choose their own leaders and run their own affairs. Yet, American weapons found their way to Belgian military bases in the Congo, and Portugal used US-supplied napalm and chemical weapons in Angola, Mozambique and Guinea. Similarly, Kennedy was the first American president to impose sanctions on South Africa to try to force an end to apartheid, but investments by US banks and multinationals in South Africa continued to increase during his administration.[2]

Finally, Africa was the continent across which containment had least hold on American policy-makers, and this had three interesting repercussions. First, it allowed a pragmatism which Kennan's original conception endorsed. In Angola and Ethiopia, it allowed the US to accept 'losses' to the West. Second, it allowed co-operation between the superpowers, either directly or implicitly. They swapped proxies in the Somali–Ethiopian conflict and, when Ford and Carter supported black majority rule in Rhodesia (Zimbabwe), they found themselves aligned with both China and the USSR. Third, the permeability of the African foreign policy agenda threw up fascinating contradictions, none more so than when the Reagan administration, after images of Ethiopian famines in the mid-1980s hit American television, became 'the largest official donor to the most doctrinaire marxist government on the African continent.'[3]

The US and the Middle East – setting the trend

The Truman administration made three lasting contributions to US Middle Eastern policy. It abandoned traditional US non-involvement, endorsed the existence of Israel, and followed a pattern of diplomatic schizophrenia that characterised American policies in the region for much of the Cold War. The Middle East initially remained low on the list of Cold War priorities, despite the fact that the 1946 dispute about the withdrawal of Soviet troops from Iran produced one of the first Cold War crises. NSC-68 changed that insofar as the US became more concerned about protecting its interests in the region. These interests were driven neither by history nor moral conviction. The Americans had no tradition of enmity with the Soviet Union in the Middle East, had little identification with the people there whose religious and socio-cultural values were very different from western liberalism, and were frequently critical of the corrupt, backward and dictatorial regimes that littered the region. Instead, US policy was justified by ideology and driven by considerations that were not necessarily Cold War related. By far the most important of these was the economic interdependence of the Western world and the Middle East. As President Eisenhower put it in 1956, they were 'together the most strategic areas in the world – Western Europe requires

Middle Eastern oil and Middle Eastern oil is of importance mainly through its contribution to the Western European economy.'⁴ What Eisenhower did not mention, but which was uppermost in American calculations, was that most of that oil was either produced by American oil companies or coveted by them. Indeed, in 1954 the Eisenhower administration was instrumental in their obtaining, at Britain's expense, a major share of the Anglo-Iranian Oil Company's (AIOC) concession in Iran.⁵ Such expansionism had Cold War justification in terms of the oil companies generating economic prosperity as a counterweight to communism and acting as stabilising forces within concession granting nations. Similarly, American geostrategic planning for the Middle East was couched in terms of denying the Soviets oil resources and potential bases from which to launch an assault upon the Persian Gulf. Nevertheless, there was no disguising the fact that American economic interests were the primary beneficiaries of US policy and that the repatriation of enormous profits from oil operations smacked heavily of neo-imperialism.

Almost as important as the new attitude towards the Middle East was Truman's intervention in the question of the Palestine Mandate. This was a British responsibility and erratic American policy sorely tested Anglo–American relations. It was also an issue heavily charged by US domestic politics. In fact, when Truman connived in the UN with the Soviets to force a partition of Palestine into Arab and Jewish states on 29 November 1947, the British Foreign Secretary, Ernest Bevin, accused him of pandering to the US domestic Jewish vote. Above all else though, Truman's was a policy that imposed enormous constraints on subsequent US administrations.

On 14 May 1948, Israel declared its independence. America and the Soviet Union hastened to recognise it but the surrounding Arab nations refused and instead launched an invasion. Egyptian, Iraqi, Lebanese, Syrian and Jordanian armies inflicted heavy casualties on Israeli forces before the US and the Soviet Union sponsored a four-week UN truce. This respite gave Israel time to buy large quantities of weapons from communist Czechoslovakia and when hostilities resumed it drove the Arab armies back deep into their own territories. By the time the US sponsored another peace deal, Israel had expanded its borders far beyond those envisaged by the original UN partition of Palestine. As a result, the Truman administration had helped bring about the creation of Israel at the enormous cost of alienating the Arab world and creating the Palestinian refugee problem. The latter was a festering sore which determined the later conduct of Middle Eastern states far more than the effects of the Cold War. Moreover, by its actions, the Truman administration compromised US ability to contain communism in the Middle East. Washington's *de facto* special relationship with Israel undermined US efforts to establish regional collective security arrangements, allowed the Soviets to champion Arab countries against Israel, and created an explosive situation. The issues involved were not of the Cold War but, nevertheless, threatened to feed off them as the proxies of the US and the USSR embroiled the superpowers in their internecine disputes. In 1956, 1967, 1973 and 1982–84, the Arab–Israeli conflict burst into open warfare with the potential to escalate wildly out of control into a major Cold War conflict.[6]

Truman's final legacy was an inchoate policy incapable of fully meeting US rhetoric and ambitions in the Middle East. There were two principal threats to Western interests: direct Soviet intervention and communist subversion from within, or at least its collusion with radical Arab nationalism, which could bring about regimes inimical to the West. The former was considered unlikely, but it still had to be catered for. As the US had little power in the region and the Pentagon was strongly averse to over-extending into the Middle East, policy-makers chose to rely upon the colonial powers of Britain and France to act as guarantors of regional security. At the same time, the US sought to align itself with Middle Eastern nationalism, which was staunchly opposed to Western colonialism, and to develop its own influence and economic interests, often at the expense of its European allies. This produced both a grossly oversimplified view of the Middle East and a debilitating kind of US diplomatic schizophrenia. Policy-makers recognised the existence of religious divides, deep social unrest and the clash between modernisation and traditionalism. They also identified the running sore of Israel within the body of Arab states, the rising tide of nationalism and the grave intra and inter state tensions – such as between Iran and Iraq, Egypt and Saudi Arabia, Turkey and Syria, Turkey and Greece, and North and South Yemen. Nevertheless, they superimposed a Cold War framework upon this complex mosaic that distorted the realities of the situation and led them to inappropriate responses. Moreover, they tried to ride three horses simultaneously – direct US economic and political expansionism, support for colonial powers, and the championing of nationalist movements. At various times these all ran in different directions and left in their wake a confusing array of inconsistent short-term decisions that defied any explanation other than expediency.[7]

From denial to surrogates

When Truman left office in January 1953, US Middle Eastern policy was already in deep trouble. Hopes that nationalism and Islam could be harnessed against communism had been replaced by fears that the communists had hijacked them first. Likewise, hopes were fading that Britain could hold its Middle Eastern position. It had withdrawn from Greece, was in dire financial straits, and under serious nationalist attack in both Iran and Egypt – the former hosted the AIOC's enormously important oil operations and the latter the bulk of Britain's Middle Eastern military presence near the geostrategically vital Suez Canal. Together with the quickening pace of decolonisation, this threatened a power vacuum in the Middle East, the loss of traditional Western bases, and great opportunities for the Soviets to expand their interests into the Persian Gulf.

Eisenhower continued established trends. Moral claims, the intellectual preferences of policy-makers and international law were all sacrificed as US fears of rampant nationalism led it to ally itself increasingly with conservative forces. In August 1953, the CIA manufactured a coup in Iran to topple the democratically elected Mohammed Mosadeq in favour, ultimately, of the autocratic Shah and his brutal police, the Savak, around whom the Americans built a client state. In January 1957, the Eisenhower Doctrine also implied a firm commitment to the existing order. For example, the US offered military aid to friendly governments and withdrew its efforts to resolve the Arab–Israeli issue; that poisoned chalice was handed to the UN. Furthermore, in July 1958, Eisenhower sent US marines to preserve the *status quo* in the Lebanon when pan-Arab radicalism threatened to spill over from the overthrow of the Hashemite monarchy of Iraq.

The Eisenhower administration also looked to regional organisations to reconcile its desire for Middle Eastern security with reduced defence budgets and the Pentagon's obsessive reluctance to commit US forces. The bulk of US expenditure went to Turkey and Iran in the hope that these, along with Pakistan, would form a Northern Tier to deter Soviet expansionism. The Americans hoped, too, to bring these countries together with Britain to co-ordinate regional defence. The basis for this was secured on 24 February 1955 with the signing of the Baghdad Pact, but a combination of the US refusal to join and intense Arab opposition meant that it ultimately failed. Iraq withdrew in March 1959, the subsequent Central Treaty Organisation (CENTO) did nothing much and, importantly, British power waned palpably.

The US had long known of British decline but had refused to act upon it because the only answer was one that American policy-makers did not want to hear – they would have to fill the power vacuum. However, the Suez Crisis brought matters to a head. On 26 July 1956, Egyptian President Gamal Abdul Nasser nationalised the Anglo–French owned Suez Canal Company. Britain and France collaborated with Israel to teach the

Egyptians a lesson. On 19 October, Israeli forces drove into the Sinai peninsular. Britain and France pressed a stage-managed ultimatum upon Israeli and Egyptian forces to withdraw from the Suez Canal Zone. Shortly afterwards, they bombed Egyptian bases, dropped paratroopers and launched an amphibious assault. Eisenhower was dismayed. The timing, on the eve of American elections, was politically embarrassing because he was running for re-election on a peace ticket. It also made it difficult to make propaganda capital of the brutal Soviet repression of the 1956 Hungarian uprising. More importantly, the Anglo–French intervention pulled the US back into the Arab–Israeli quagmire. The US could not be seen to support blatantly the forces of colonialism. Nor did it want to forfeit the goodwill it had been trying to regain with the Arab states by siding with Israel. Furthermore, it did not want to give the Soviets a pretext for intervention. Eisenhower decided to prioritise US Cold War concerns over the vested interests of his major allies and applied sufficient economic and diplomatic pressure to force Britain and France to withdraw. However, this was not before the Soviets had won a Third World propaganda coup by brandishing their atomic weapons at the imperialist Western powers.

Although the Eisenhower administration scored some short-term successes, notably in Iran, it left a power vacuum in the Middle East which it had first tried to ignore, particularly with regard to the waning British position, and had then made things worse by humiliating Britain and France over Suez. The short-lived Kennedy administration achieved little and it fell to Presidents Johnson and Nixon to deal with the problem. Both were preoccupied with Vietnam and realised that the US could ill-afford a sufficient build-up of power to play a balancing role in the Indian Ocean and Persian Gulf. However, neither could they indulge themselves in the illusion that Britain could fill a regional power vacuum. This became self-evident in 1968 when it announced its intent to withdraw its military forces from east of Suez. The US now resorted increasingly to the use of surrogates to hold the *status quo*.

Interestingly, the US used both state and non-state actors. Of the latter, by far the most important were the US oil companies operating in the Middle East. These, such as the Arabian–American Oil Company in Saudi Arabia, held privileged positions that made them effectively ambassadors of the West. They also became vehicles through which, using powerful tax incentives, US administrations could channel foreign aid without congressional approval.[8] State surrogates were often less compliant, but more numerous. In the Six Day War in 1967, Johnson moved US policy decisively toward supporting Israel against the Arabs. In a brilliant military campaign, the Israelis inflicted a humiliating defeat upon the Arab states. Johnson made no attempt to force an Israeli withdrawal. Instead, he sponsored UN resolution 242, which proposed a land for peace deal whereby Israel would return occupied territory in exchange for security guarantees, and in December 1968 he supplied Israel with F-4 Phantom jets. Nixon's approach took the idea of using surrogates even further as he developed the Twin Pillar strategy whereby Iran and Saudi Arabia would police the Persian Gulf. To facilitate this and, conveniently, to help the ailing American economy, the US sold them vast quantities of sophisticated weaponry. In 1972, Nixon told the Shah that he could purchase any non-nuclear weapons and in 1974 alone, the Foreign Military Sales (FMS) agreement saw the US supply him with over $3950 million of arms. Similar offers were made to Saudi Arabia. In 1975, US–Saudi FMS agreements were worth almost $5776 million and later that year Secretary of State Kissinger persuaded President Ford to allow it to purchase F-15 fighters.

Out of the ashes

American hopes that surrogates would be able to guarantee regional stability proved to be short-lived as the 1970s struck their Middle Eastern policy a series of blows. Three stand out in particular. The first came in 1973 when the Yom Kippur War erupted. Egypt and Syria, with Soviet backing, attacked Israel and won a series of stunning victories. The US supplied Israel with replacement arms necessary to repel Arab forces and, by 15 October, the Israelis had reversed the situation and were poised to annihilate the Egyptian Third Army. The Soviets announced their intent to intervene militarily, either as part of a combined operation with the US or unilaterally. However, the Americans saw this as a pretext for the Soviets to establish a foothold in the region. Accordingly, Nixon put US nuclear forces on alert and NSA Henry Kissinger pushed through UN resolution 338 that called for the full implementation of UN resolution 242. Ultimately, another begrudging peace was restored, but by then the spirit of *détente* and the American position had incurred serious damage. Contrary to the 1972 US–Soviet summit declarations, the US had pursued unilateral advantage and demonstrated its unwillingness to treat the Soviets as an equal in the Middle East. Also, US championship of Israel against the Arab world had serious consequences. It damaged the Atlantic alliance because the US failed to secure the support of its NATO allies for its action, most of them being disenchanted with the intolerant Israeli attitude and preoccupied with their need for Arab oil. It also awakened the Arab states to the power that their oil afforded them against the US, which by 1973 had become a net importer of oil. The

Organisation of Arab Petroleum Exporting Countries imposed an oil embargo on supporters of Israel, notably the US and the Netherlands. It imposed, too, a crippling price hike on oil which threw Western Europe's economy into chaos and ruined early attempts at Economic and Monetary Union. The only real consolation for the US was that its resolute action persuaded Egyptian leaders that it would never allow Israel to be destroyed and, therefore, that their flirtation with the Soviets would bring them less reward than would an improved relationship with Washington.

Two further blows were struck to US Middle Eastern policy in 1979. First, the Soviets dealt a fatal blow to *détente* and threatened to destabilise the region when they invaded Afghanistan. The subsequent Carter Doctrine heralded a new hardline, warning as it did that the US would take military action to keep the Soviets away from the Persian Gulf. Meantime, Carter imposed economic sanctions on the USSR and the CIA began covert support of Afghan resistance fighters. Second, the fundamentalist Ayatollah Khomeini led the Iranian revolution that deprived the US of one of its closest collaborators and destroyed the Twin Pillar strategy. In fact, the US reaped the rewards of an Iranian policy that had been de-legitimised from the moment the CIA toppled Mosadeq in August 1953. Successive presidents championed an Iranian regime bent upon popular repression and by doing so sacrificed the democratic aspirations of a nation to a Cold War threat that was more imagined than real. Thereafter, in the most intensely media-covered US foreign policy crisis of all time, Iran humiliated the Carter administration during the bungled attempt to rescue American embassy staff held hostage in Teheran. Just as importantly, Iran became an embittered bastion of anti-Americanism, a haven for what the US labelled terrorists, and a focal point for Islamic fundamentalism and anti-imperial fanaticism.[9]

Although there were differences in rhetoric, the policies of US administrations from Nixon through to Reagan were consistent. All of them made efforts to rebuild the tattered US relationship with the Arab states. Kissinger's shuttle diplomacy during 1973–74 succeeded in stopping the Middle East war and beginning the peace process.[10] Capitalising upon President Sadat's move away from the Soviets, President Carter mediated the Camp David Accords that led in March 1979 to an Egyptian–Israeli peace treaty. Whereas on many issues Carter's idealism and concern for human rights ran foul of US national security considerations, this was undoubtedly his greatest foreign policy success.[11] Likewise, in 1988 the US began to tackle the Palestinian problem once the PLO leader, Yasser Arafat, had finally accepted UN resolution 242 and the legal existence of Israel.

All administrations sought, too, to preserve America's established pattern of allies in the Middle East, most notably with the Saudis and the Israelis. In the immediate aftermath of the Yom Kippur War, the US provided the latter with more than $3 billion of weapons. In the early 1980s, Washington also turned a blind eye to Israel's invasion of the Lebanon in the hope that this would bring them into conflict with Syria, which was regarded as a Soviet client state. Furthermore, there was an increasing willingness to combat Middle Eastern terrorism, particularly after the ill-fated deployment of a US peace-making force of marines in 1982 to Beruit resulted in 241 men being killed in a truck bomb attack. The best known example of this determination was Reagan's air strike in April 1986 against Quadaffi's Libya.

The single most important development in US Middle Eastern policy, though, was its move away from reliance on either colonial or indigenous allies. The collapse of imperial power and the Twin Pillar strategy gave impetus to a major ongoing review of US policy in the Indian Ocean and Persian Gulf. Nationalism, fundamentalism, decolonisation and communist machinations meant that land bases were increasingly unreliable and temporary assets. From Nixon onwards, US emphasis was on sea and air power, particularly once the wind-down in Vietnam released materials and the Yom Kippur War emphasised the need for military guarantees of precious oil shipments. In 1980, the Carter Doctrine committed the US to military action should any force seek to control the Persian Gulf and frantic efforts were made to back this promise with credible firepower. The island of Diego Garcia became the focal point of an enormous expansion of US capabilities in the Indian Ocean area and a Rapid Reaction Force was created to fight 'brush-fires', the funding for which Reagan increased by 85% – an additional $2 billion. In fact, Caspar Weinberger confirmed that from lowly beginnings the Middle East had, by the time that the Cold War closed, finally achieved 'top-billing' in US security considerations. As far as Reagan's Defence Secretary was concerned, the Persian Gulf had become the centre of conflict for the foreseeable future.[12]

Conclusion

US policy-makers struggled throughout the Cold War to manage their relationships with Africa and the Middle East. The latter was by far the more pressing. There the Americans variously deluded themselves by relying upon European imperial power that simply was no longer sufficient, developed surrogates to fight their battles for them, and finally accepted the burden of building-up the force necessary to arbitrate the balance of power in the Indian Ocean and Persian Gulf. In the process they toppled progressive governments, supported dictators, turned a blind eye to Israeli atrocities in the Lebanon and, when it suited them, abandoned their closest allies, as with Britain and France during the Suez Crisis. The lens of containment through which policy-makers so often viewed the region distorted its problems into zero sum calculations of profit or loss *vis-à-vis* the Soviets. The concern above all else was the economic dependence of the Western world on Middle Eastern oil. The US therefore emphasised military security and, too often, the preservation of the *status quo* to protect Western, not Middle Eastern, interests. Indeed, its treatment of progressive and infant democracies raises significant issues regarding both the conduct of US foreign policy and the currently popular democratic peace theory (see Chapter 10).

It is ironic that the Americans practised containment better in Africa than in the Middle East. In fact, it was precisely because the US cared less for Africa that policy-makers were, in relative terms at least, freed from the constraints of 'cult containment' to practise the flexible version proposed by Kennan. For example, Carter's sanction of a 'loss' in Somalia in 1978 and quiet acceptance of a twenty-year Treaty of Friendship and Co-operation concluded subsequently between Ethiopia and the USSR would have been unthinkable in other parts of the world. However, the mantle of US moral supremacy was no less tarnished here than elsewhere. American arms facilitated proxy and civil wars that soaked Africa in the blood of countless thousands and, as American leaders poured out rhetoric stressing the plight of Black Africa, their actions and US economic interests underwrote white supremacy in South Africa.

It is interesting that three similarities between the US experience in Africa and in the Middle East help explain some of the problems policy-makers faced and the sometimes inappropriate nature of their actions. First, the US most probably made the problems of Africa and the Middle East, and thus of itself, much worse. Its quest for stability led successive American presidents to sponsor regimes that denied the peoples of these regions those rights and freedoms for which the US stood. Similarly, the substitution of American economic expansionism for collapsing imperial power, especially in the Middle East, created a new form of dependency and another focal point for extremist agitation, and the use of proxies justified the supply of vast quantities of arms which caused carnage to no Cold War end. Second, both regions demonstrated the blurring of US foreign and domestic policy. This was evident in the Middle East with the Jewish lobby, but was also particularly pronounced in Africa, where the lack of US strategic interests allowed a more flexible agenda. Thus, African policy more than any other Cold War theatre

concern for oil, Arab–Israeli tension, and a number of states hostile to the US, such as Libya, Syria, and Iran. Finally, in the Western Hemisphere, the US faced economic, political, and security challenges including Castro's Cuba, Noriega's Panama, drug trafficking and renewed charges of neo-imperialism.

All of this needs to be borne in mind as the inconsistency, *ad hoc* arrangements, and gap between New World Order rhetoric and reality in American foreign policy becomes apparent. Have Bush and Clinton betrayed the hopes of the post-Cold War generation for a New World Order? Has America, as the last superpower, shirked its international responsibilities and continued the double standards it so readily justified by containment? Or, as Mearsheimer has suggested, have we gone 'back to the future' to a situation vastly more complex than the Cold War, possibly more dangerous, and certainly offering more problems than solutions?[1]

Europe

President Bush set the tone of the American relationship with the EC (EU after ratification of the Maastricht Treaty in November 1993) and its member states with his famous 'beef hormone and pasta' speech which portrayed the two sides as locked into competitive co-operation. As a zone of stability and economic strength Washington appreciated the EU as an integral partner, and Bush never wavered from the difficult diplomatic task of facilitating the reunification of Germany in 1990, which then indisputably became the heart of the EU. The economic fortunes of the two remained intertwined and the significance of transatlantic relations has been elevated to new heights with the launch of the euro in January 1999, economic volatility in Asia, and the development of the WTO. The EU has also remained an essential partner in providing for, and sharing the burden of, European security. To this end, Bush and Clinton have endorsed deeper and wider European integration. Security concerns in Central and Eastern European Countries (CEECs) were predominantly economic, which meant that the EU could help substantially through enlargement to include CEECs and assistance packages such as the PHARE programme[2] and Technical Assistance to the Commonwealth of Independent States (TACIS). Deeper integration has also allowed the US to develop its special relationship with Germany in the knowledge that it remains 'contained' by NATO membership and by new European policies such as EMU and a Common Foreign and Security Policy (CFSP). Furthermore, the Americans have broadly welcomed the development of a European Security and Defence Identity (ESDI) based around the WEU and CFSP. Early caution lest ESDI rival NATO has been assuaged both by members of Eurocorps conceding that NATO can have first-call on it for Article 5 missions (i.e. those within NATO jurisdiction) and by a French rapprochement with NATO, albeit that France has not yet re-entered its military command structure. Clinton has consequently embraced initiatives such as the Combined Joint Task Force in 1994 as means for maintaining American leadership whilst at the same time burden-sharing and increasing US freedom of manoeuvre.

However, the end of the Cold War has also produced new transatlantic tensions because Europe perceives less reason either to surrender to US economic sensitivities or to follow its lead in security matters. Both sides have recognised the dangers inherent in this. Hence they have agreed measures such as the Transatlantic Declaration of November 1990, which reaffirmed EC–US determination to strengthen their partnership; the New Transatlantic Agenda in December 1995, which committed them to work together in almost 100 policy areas; and prospectively a 'Millennium Round' of talks to examine their trade differences. Such palliatives, though, have not prevented a long series of economic problems from erupting over environmental policies, economic sanctions against Cuba, industrial, agricultural and cultural (films) protectionism, and preferential trade agreements. The latter, in 1999, caused the tragi-comical 'banana war'. These problems have been compounded by a weakening of the transatlantic coincidence of security interests, and by a necessary revision of institutions now that the Soviet threat has gone. The US has supported the continuation and adjustment of NATO as its principal claim to leadership in Europe, but, in relative terms, has downgraded the region in favour of the Middle East and Asia. The European powers have supported NATO's adjustment as a way to lock in an American contribution to European security but have also developed other fora that may challenge US leadership. The potential for conflict is clear. The so-called Dobbins *Démarche*[3] of February 1991 stated US opposition to the development of the WEU outside of NATO but there is no certainty that this will not happen given European commitment to an effective CFSP. Likewise, there are transatlantic and intra-European differences over the role of the Organisation for Security and Co-operation in Europe and the issue of NATO enlargement, which some fear will alienate Russia. Moreover, reduced levels of transatlantic cohesion have been demonstrated by the Bosnian crisis. Here, US equivocation further damaged what hopes remained for assertive multilateralism. The credibility of both US leadership and of NATO was placed in question. Indeed, the tardiness with which the US sponsored the Dayton Accords in 1995 to settle the conflict, and

Clinton's undercutting of European initiatives such as the Vance–Owen Peace Plan and a UN arms embargo, have led some to conclude that it 'was as if there was a need to demonstrate that the Europeans could not succeed without US help … '.[4]

This is not to suggest that the US is friendless in Europe, far from it. Clinton has good personal relationships with key European leaders, has strengthened the Anglo–American relationship with Prime Minister Tony Blair, and secured political respect for his stalwart support of Senator Mitchell's prolonged but successful mediation of the Northern Ireland peace process in 1999. Even more importantly, a speedy and more assertive response to President Milosevic's ethnic cleansing in Kosovo in 1999 has partially redeemed NATO and American leadership in Europe. On 24 March, NATO began Operation Allied Force, a massive air campaign designed to bomb Serbia into submission. On 3 June, after an air offensive spanning 77 days, Milosevic accepted NATO terms and the United Nations, backed by 50,000 troops of the Kosovo Implementation Force (KFOR), moved in to attempt to construct democratic self-rule in Kosovo.

Nevertheless, challenges remain for the US, particularly in the Balkans where winning the peace may well prove harder than winning the wars. Thus far Dayton has failed in its aim to create a multiethnic, democratic, and economically sustainable Bosnia. Kosovo remains blighted by revenge attacks against Serbs, and its security depends upon KFOR. This implies another long-term commitment, which former NATO Secretary General Solana pledged but that US and other Western governments will have to justify paying for. More trouble might also be looming, this time in Montenegro where President Djukanovic is pushing increasingly for independence of Milosevic's Yugoslav federation. Not only does this raise the question of Belgrade's reaction but also, if Montenegro achieved independence, the likelihood of renewed pressure for Kosovo independence and a potential chain reaction that might destabilise the whole region.[5]

Washington might draw comfort from the fact that increasing difficulties with its European Cold War allies and within the Balkans can be addressed in the context of underlying friendship and mutual dependence. The same cannot be said of its other big European problem: the Soviet Union/Russia. President Bush looked initially to use the UN in tandem with Soviet co-operation to fashion a post-Cold War world order, led by America, but with others sharing the burden. However, his Soviet policy was thrown into turmoil in mid-1991 when an old guard backlash rocked Gorbachev. He survived an attempted coup in August, but his efforts to preserve the communist party and the USSR were doomed to failure. By January 1992, he and the Soviet Union had left the world stage and Bush was left to preside over America's unipolar moment.

This was more difficult to deal with than Gorbachev. Soviet collapse was an earthquake in the geostrategic topography of Europe that reduced the commonality of American–Soviet/Russian interest in the *status quo*. Where once there was a stabilising force, led by a tested leader anxious to develop good relations with the West, there stood an unstable Russia surrounded by numerous newly independent states, each keen to press their national interests. Moreover, Russia's new leader, Boris Yeltsin, was an untested and ostensibly more radical democratic leader than Gorbachev. He was also surrounded at home by rising nationalism and disillusionment with market reform and confronted abroad by both a security vacuum between Russia and a powerful re-unified Germany and a need to stabilise the Russian periphery, the so-called 'Near Abroad'. By the end of 1992, despite signing a second START treaty, receiving American funds under the October 1992 Freedom Support Act and seeing Russia admitted to the IMF in June, Yeltsin had moved Russia away from Gorbachev's partnership approach to the US in favour of a more assertive policy.

In the 1992 US presidential election, Clinton condemned Bush for not supporting Yeltsin earlier, for betraying the rights to self-determination of the peoples in the Soviet Union, and for a lack of imagination which threatened to lose America the Cold War peace.[6] Such claims are unconvincing. Bush did what numerous American leaders have done in times of uncertainty. He built upon the *status quo* and embraced a regime that ran contrary to American principles because it was in America's interest to do so. Equally unconvincing have been Clinton's own efforts to fulfil election pledges to deliver a strategic partnership with Russia and international leadership to the world. Ambivalence rather than imagination characterised US foreign policy in Clinton's first year. The Republicans laid the foundation of his $2.5 billion aid programme for Russia in 1993/94.[7] Concessions from the West on rescheduling Russia's foreign debt were scarcely revolutionary. And his decision to mortgage US Russian policy to Boris Yeltsin's ability to deliver successful domestic reform was little different to Bush's reliance upon Gorbachev to hold the Soviet Union together.

Clinton subsequently revised the policy that fell haplessly between his idealism and Bush's pragmatism. Strategic partnership has been quietly shelved in favour of a twofold plan to secure a less ambitious normalisation of US–Russian relations. First, the US continued its support of both Yeltsin, despite his faltering leadership, and international efforts to stabilise Russia. There were no alternatives. In December 1993, the ultra nationalist Liberal Democratic Party led by Vladimir Zhirinovsky captured 25% of the vote and, in 1995, the communists staged a remarkable comeback to take 22% of the vote and over one-third of the seats in the Lower House. On this score it was illuminating to note the marked absence of Clinton's rhetoric about human rights when Yeltsin invaded Chechnya in December 1994, an attitude very reminiscent of Bush's pragmatism when Soviet troops were dispatched to Azerbaijan in January 1990. Second, the US took further precautions to guard against either a resurgent Russia or the effects of its weakness. Foremost amongst these measures has been the controversial enlargement of NATO and efforts to mollify Russian security concerns with the 'Partnership for Peace' and the NATO–Russia Founding Act of May 1997. In addition, the relationship with the Ukraine is being developed as a counterweight to a future expansion of Russian power and several initiatives have been taken to prevent 'accidents'. These include nuclear 'de-targeting' and improved control over stockpiles, and the Nunn–Lugar program, which provides $400 million annually to tackle the problems of Russia's ageing nuclear reactors and avert another Chernobyl disaster.

Nevertheless, there is no disguising that the American–Russian relationship has cooled significantly since 1990. The US, both public and private, remains reluctant to invest in a Russia plagued by corruption and instability. In 1998 the economy collapsed, the largest financial assistance package in IMF history, some $17.1 billion, was squandered, and the Managing Director of the IMF, Michel Camdessus, launched a scathing attack on the 'crony capitalism' that costs Russia $15 billion per annum in corruption. Trust between Washington and the Kremlin is also weakening. Clinton's impeachment proceedings cast doubts upon his integrity whilst Russia's leadership and incipient democracy remain in bewildering flux. Twice during 1999 Yeltsin sacked governments for no clear reason, and on 31 December he dramatically announced his own resignation. Furthermore, differences have mounted: Russian conduct in the 'Near Abroad' and sale of nuclear technology to states embargoed by America, such as Iran; the West's intervention in Bosnia; Russia's dissatisfaction with the 1990 CFE treaty; and the 'economic imperialism' of IMF criteria. Most recently, two issues have highlighted the growing tension. First, the Kremlin was disturbed by the American-led NATO military action against Serbia during 1999. Their countermove was to send a symbolic Russian force into Kosovo to occupy Pristina airport and to curtail NATO–Russia dialogue in the Permanent Joint Council, which had been set up after the Founding Act. Second, the messy compromise that ended the humiliating Chechen War in August 1996, whereby Chechnya acted *de facto* as an independent territory, collapsed in 1999. Russia is currently waging a war of revenge that is enormously popular at home and refuses to bow to international pressure to stop its military advance upon the capital Grozny. Yeltsin even crudely reminded Clinton that Russia still has nuclear weapons.

It has been suggested that 'Far from having the *wrong* policy toward Russia, the United States may cease to have one at all.'[8] This is an exaggeration, but it is a bitter irony that US policy-makers have found Russian weakness more difficult than Russian strength, and that Gorbachev's communist Soviet Union perhaps offered a better prospect of strategic partnership than 'democratic' Russia. Today, the future of US–Russia relations is perhaps more uncertain than at any time since the end of the Cold War. Yeltsin's resignation ushers in a new era of relations that begins in inauspicious times. US intervention in Bosnia and Kosovo and its criticism of the Chechen campaign have stirred anti-American sentiment in Russian public opinion. Also, Yeltsin's allegedly soft approach to the West was under increasing attack from Russian industrial and military leaders. Moreover, current Prime Minister and Presidential front-runner Vladimir Putin, an ex-KGB officer, is resolved upon a popular hardline in the Caucasus. In such circumstances, whoever wins the presidential election on 26 March 2000 may well adopt a harder line toward the US and pursue other foreign policy options. Indeed, Putin has already worked carefully to play on US–European differences, and former Prime Minister Primakov has talked openly of a strategic triangle of Russia, India and China to counterbalance the US.

Asia

Asia was the nemesis of Cold War US foreign policy: Vietnam was its epitome. In the 1990s the threat has been different but little easier to deal with. Asia's long history of instability posed new problems as rapid economic growth in the 1980s and early 1990s allowed many of its countries to modernise their military capabilities. Major US concerns on this score include North Korean nuclear ambitions, Chinese claims in the North China Sea, and the long-running saga of Taiwan. Potentially dangerous cultural, religious and economic divisions have also emerged, both between Asia and the US and within Asia. Malay and Indonesian reformers have embraced a revitalised Islamic identity and there have been major tensions about disproportionate Chinese commercial influence, most notably in Indonesia where, in 1998, the Chinese totalled 4% of the population, but controlled 80% of the assets of the top three hundred companies. Similarly, anti-Western imperialist sentiment was inflamed when Australian troops led a UN peacekeeping mission into East Timor in 1999. Furthermore, economic globalisation and the redefinition of the security agenda have caused Asia to pose a twofold challenge to the US. First, as the Asian tiger economies boomed, they challenged US economic interests and influence. Second, when they went into spiralling recession, shockwaves were felt throughout the world's financial markets and US fears of Asian protectionism grew.

American responses have been characterised by Defence Secretary Richard Cheney as a 'balancing wheel' role in Asia.[9] However, this has become increasingly difficult in the absence of bipolar discipline and with relative US economic decline. Bush and more especially Clinton have supported regional co-operation through organisations such as the Association of South East Asian Nations (ASEAN) but have also aggressively and unilaterally pursued US economic interests. An APEC meeting in November 1998 revealed increasing tension between the eastern and western edges of the Pacific. More difficult still for America was widespread sympathy for Dr Mahathir, Malaysia's Prime Minister, as he warned at the meeting of the dangers for Asia posed by too much economic liberalisation. This has clashed, and continues to clash, with US determination to prise open Asian markets by setting ambitious targets for trade liberalisation and exporting American/IMF-style capitalism.

This conflict of interests has been particularly pronounced with Japan, America's foremost Asian ally. Japan and the US remain 'inextricably intertwined, economically, politically, and militarily.'[10] Nevertheless, the end of the Cold War has both partly liberated Japan from its dependence on US military guarantees and forced it to take a more assertive international role. At the 1995 Osaka summit of APEC, Tokyo split with the US over the pace and style of economic liberalisation in East Asia. This is problematic for American strategy, especially as Japan's share of the Asian market has grown more rapidly than that of the US. Another important factor in their cooling relationship has been the aggression with which Clinton has attacked Japan's 'closed' market and the fortitude with which the Japanese have defended it. The Bush approach to Japan was moderate, talking of voluntary import expansion targets (VIE) but careful not to antagonise the Japanese government. Clinton has had a different approach, signalled by 'hawkish' appointments such as Mickey Kantor as USTR and Lawrence Summers as Deputy Secretary of the Treasury. In February 1994, the Hosokawa summit became deadlocked as Japan resisted American demands to deregulate and to expand its imports. Matters hit a flashpoint in the 1995 'car crisis'. The preceding year the auto and auto parts industry accounted for 58% of America's $66 billion trade deficit with Japan, equivalent to 23% of the total global US trade deficit. Clinton threatened 100% punishment tariffs on thirteen models of Japanese car if Japan did not accede to US VIE demands. Such assertive US unilateralism was clearly at odds with its declared support for multilateralism. More importantly, Japan refused to buckle and, although some points of compromise were eventually reached, the American assault caused such damage to American–Japanese relations that US trade policy here has been described as 'almost a disaster area'.[11]

American–Japanese tensions in trade have been mirrored in their security relationship. In 1995 the US Defence Department released a report 'United States Strategy for the East Asia Pacific Region', which stressed the importance of Japanese co-operation. The Americans were therefore heartened by Japan's 'Modality' report in 1994, which reaffirmed its strategic alliance with the US. But Japan remains reluctant to shoulder the burdens America expects of it. This was demonstrated in October 1995 when its Self-Defence Agency recommended cuts of 10-20% in Japan's defence forces. More important still, even though China still worries them both, America and Japan no longer share such an identity of security interests now that the Soviet threat has gone. Traditional Japanese reluctance to participate in foreign affairs is changing and, as former Prime Minister Morihiro Hosokawa has argued, global conditions force Japan to play a greater international role. Moreover, a new generation of political leaders, less affected by the legacy of the Second World War, is looking to develop a more independent Japanese role; hence Japan's contribution to recent UN peacekeeping missions in Cambodia, Mozambique and Rwanda. Within this new Japanese perspective, reliance on the US has become less essential. In fact, as the priority given to military security gives way to economic security, the US actually poses as many problems as it helps solve. With a GDP of over 507 trillion yen, and a population of more than 126 million, Japan is a reasonably secure regional power. Indeed, Japan's leaders are very conscious that any concerted move to strengthen their military capability might decrease their security by provoking others into an arms race. Besides, they can take for granted US protection if China, the other regional power, were to make aggressive moves in Asia. Furthermore, symbols of Japan's continuing reliance on the US are becoming increasingly unpopular amongst the Japanese public. In this respect, the gang-rape of a teenage girl by American servicemen on Okinawa has been particularly damaging. In 1995 public support for the US security treaty fell to 42% and in 1997 the Japanese ranked the US as a threat second only to Korea.

The US balancing role in Asia has been complicated further by China, the country singled out in 1996 by Warren Christopher as an increasingly important market and as being potentially decisive in tipping the balance

Africa and, within this, US assistance to South Africa exceeded all other African countries combined. Furthermore, Clinton's notions of 'selective engagement' have largely failed to clarify the policies inherited from and developed since the Bush years. There is an unwillingness to become militarily involved in Africa again. This was reflected in September 1993 when Clinton spoke to the UN about criteria for future interventions: clear mission objectives, palpable danger to international peace, a clear exit strategy, and calculable costs. This message was reinforced when public opinion reacted with hostility to the deaths of eighteen US soldiers in Somalia in October 1993, and again in 1994 when Congress terminated funding for operations there and rendered the US embarrassingly impotent when mass genocide reached its peak in Rwanda later that year. However, the same public opinion that opposes large foreign aid programmes and military intervention has responded strongly to sustained media images of human rights abuse and famine. This was reflected in the mushrooming of short-term relief assistance given in the early 1990s when Rwanda and Somalia dominated the headlines. This situation justifies two conclusions. First, the prosecution of American policy in Africa remains confused because it is unclear when, how, where, and even if, the US will intervene. Second, the general thrust of US policy indicates that no amount of American values or humanitarian concern has prevented the Bush and Clinton administrations from marginalising the vast majority of Africa as much in US policy as in the global economy.

The contrast between US attitudes to Africa and the Middle East is stark. It was never in doubt that the US would remain intimately involved in the Middle East after the Cold War. Its concern remained for oil supplies, its special relationship with Israel, to promote trade, and to guard American allies from regional rivals. In addition, there emerged new considerations such as state-sponsored terrorism, the proliferation of weapons of mass destruction, and the growing power of Islamic fundamentalism. Furthermore, it was widely acknowledged that a US retreat from its role as regional power broker could badly destabilise the Middle East. The key question was how Washington would fulfil this role and with what level of commitment.

The post-Cold War American approach to securing geostrategic stability has been the dual containment of Iran and Iraq coupled with sponsorship of the Middle Eastern peace process and the cultivation of links with moderate Arab states. In this the US has been helped considerably by two factors. First, the Iran–Iraq war that broke out in September 1980 prompted Saudi Arabia and vulnerable mini-states of the Gulf to draw closer to the US. Second, the collapse of the Cold War ended the baffling juxtaposition of great power rivalry and internecine dispute. Soviet collapse meant that the forces of opposition to America were considerably weakened by the loss of their principal benefactor. Also, new relationships became possible, such as with Syria, and the US was able to exert more pressure on Israel in the peace process because the Israelis knew that their geostrategic value to Washington had declined with the end of the Cold War.

Ironically, a miscalculation by the Bush administration encouraged the first true test of post-Cold War US commitment to the Middle East. Fear of Iran's Shiite revolution caused the Americans to favour Iraq in the Iran–Iraq war, and even after the conflict ended in August 1988 they continued to provide it with loans and access to high technology in the complacent belief that they could 'tame' Saddam Hussein. The Bush administration got it wrong. On 2 August 1990, Iraq invaded Kuwait and the Gulf War became inevitable. The speed, nature and intensity of the US response have caused great discussion. Was it motivated by concern for oil, human rights, non-proliferation of weapons of mass destruction, territorial integrity of Kuwait, or by revenge for Saddam Hussein's 'betrayal'? Most probably there were elements of all these factors. Even more importantly, in the short-term, US leadership of an international coalition operating under UN auspices to repel Iraq lent credence both to American determination to safeguard Middle Eastern stability and to hopes for assertive multilateralism and a New World Order. In the longer term, it has created an on-going test of American will and demonstrated the difficulties of holding together international collaboration. Iraq has repeatedly obstructed UN weapons inspectors and when the US took action in the winter of 1998, the lack of international support was conspicuous.

Beyond intervention against Iraq, Bush and especially Clinton have adopted a more 'low profile' American approach to the Middle East. Nowhere has this been more noticeable than in the Middle Eastern peace process, the prospects for which were improved by both the Gulf War and by the PLO's loss of Moscow's assistance. In October 1991, Bush convened the Madrid Conference, which brought all the major Middle Eastern parties together, to initiate a series of bilateral and multilateral talks aimed at reaching a comprehensive Middle Eastern peace settlement. In September 1993, Clinton presided over a momentous meeting at the White House between the PLO's chairman Yasser Arafat and Israeli Prime Minister Yitzhak Rabin. The PLO acknowledged Israel's right to exist in peace in return for Israel recognising the PLO as the official representative of the Palestinian people, allowing Palestinians in the Gaza Strip and Jericho on the West Bank to begin self-government. This was followed in 1994 by another historic meeting at the White House, this time between Rabin and King Hussein of Jordan, which provided for the normalisation of Israeli–Jordanian relations.

Since then, steps toward peace have faltered. American efforts have not been helped by Palestinian suspicions of US bias because of its close ties with Israel and the political power of the US Jewish lobby. More important have been the deep-seated nature of the dispute and the attentions of extremist groups such as Hezbollah, Hamas and Islamic Jihad. In November 1995, Yitzhak Rabin was assassinated for his part in the peace process. His replacement, Shimon Peres, put security before peace. In January 1996, the Israeli secret service assassinated 'The Engineer', Yehiya Ayash, who was a legendary Islamic terrorist and responsible for the deaths of dozens of Israelis. This move almost totally derailed the peace process because assassinating Ayash in Gaza could not have been more provocative to Palestinians and more problematic for Arafat's efforts to control Islamic militants. Peres responded to waves of retaliatory bus bombings with both the harshest blockade ever on Palestinians in the West Bank and Gaza and, in April 1996, 'Operation Grapes of Wrath', a military operation against civilian areas in southern Lebanon. The aim was to punish Hezbollah fighters but the ensuing massacre appalled world opinion and tarnished US peace mediation efforts because of its association with Israel. Subsequently, the US stepped up its efforts to control the upsurge in violence. Constant 'hand-holding' by a State Department peace team headed by Dennis Ross and interventions by Secretary of State Albright finally brought Arafat and Peres' successor, Binyamin Netanyahu, to revive the peace process. On 23 October 1998, the two signed the Wye Memorandum in Washington. However, important though this was, it left key ambiguities and the even more important problem that popular trust in the Middle Eastern peace process is still lacking.

Despite the efforts of Bush and Clinton, the quest for Arab–Israeli peace, the so-called 'Holy Grail of the American presidency',[14] still lies beyond reach, and may well have been complicated further by the death in 1999 of Jordan's respected and influential King Hussein. Likewise, although Netanyahu's successor, Ehud Barac, has encouragingly promised to withdraw Israeli troops from the Lebanon within a year, it remains to be seen how he works with Washington in the Middle East peace process. Wider dangers of violence proliferating have also increased substantially due to intra- and extra-regional developments. Iraq is almost certain to develop weapons of mass destruction in defiance of the UN and the US, and there is a strong danger that destabilising nuclear rivalry in South East Asia between India and Pakistan might spill over into the Middle East. Both countries conducted missile tests in April 1999, have refused to sign the Non Proliferation and Comprehensive Test Ban treaties, and have established relationships with rival countries in the Middle East. A further problem arises from the 'clash of civilisations' thesis whereby it is claimed that the US faces increasing difficulties in responding to the rise of Islamic fundamentalism. For example, Clinton incurred the wrath of the Muslim world in 1998 when, in reprisal for the bombing of American embassies in Africa, he launched cruise missiles against 'terrorist' sites in Afghanistan and Sudan. Finally, Clinton faces an ongoing implementation problem. It is all very well to maintain an 'over the horizon' military presence and to pursue the dual containment of Iran and Iraq, but this requires the support of allies and of the American people, neither of which is assured. Arab states of the Gulf have reduced their support for US enforcement of UN resolutions against Iraq, a move which reflects concern about a US double standard caused by its much softer approach towards Israel. Moreover, the power of the American Jewish lobby precludes a more even-handed US approach and popular concern for pressing domestic reform has debilitated presidential ability to use foreign aid to buy America much needed support in the Middle East.

Western Hemisphere

If notions of US hegemony ever held credence, then the Western Hemisphere traditionally provided their strongest support. However, Cold War collapse has removed the justification for aggressive US policies and made it more difficult to deflect charges of neo-imperialism. The situation is volatile. Fledgling democracies flounder amid right-wing resistance, enormous economic disparities, massive external debt, and in the face of recent natural disasters, such as the hurricane that ripped through Honduras and catastrophic mudslides in Venezuela. There are also huge problems to be faced in trying to develop regional co-operation at the same time as integrating very different economies into the global economy.

Washington's strategy changed little with the end of the Cold War. The emphasis remained on democratisation, market reform, integrating the region into the global economy and, more cynically, preserving US economic and political predominance. In all of these things the US has achieved some success, despite its policies being complicated by increasingly voluble domestic demands. The centrepiece of Bush and Clinton's approach has been NAFTA and subsequent promises to extend it into a hemispheric free trade area. Within this scheme Mexico was targeted to demonstrate the virtues of the 'American way'. If Mexico's internal reform and closer ties with the US were seen to work, then it would catalyse other reform-minded states to follow suit. Despite the Mexican peso crisis in 1995, which required the US to rescue it with a $40 billion package of loan guarantees, NAFTA has brought political and economic rewards, particularly since agreement was reached in 1994 to establish a free trade area of the Americas by 2005. As anticipated, it has acted as a stimulant for regional co-operation and a general, if rather slow, move toward freer trade. The hemisphere has become by far the fastest growing US export market and between 1991 and 1995 Latin America reduced its trade barriers by 80%. Also Mercosur, a free trade agreement between Brazil, Argentina, Uruguay and Paraguay, has been established, along with a similar style Andean Pact. Political co-operation has also been galvanised, notably between traditional rivals Brazil and Argentina. They have reduced defence expenditure and, in the 1990 Foz do Iguazu declaration, ceased their nuclear weapons programmes. Moreover, Brazil has taken over from Mexico as the economy *par exemplar*, despite being the country perhaps most affected by the debt crisis. Since the introduction of the *real plan* by President Cardoso in July 1994, Brazil has sustained moderate economic growth. It has also achieved an unprecedented low inflation of 3% in 1998, attracted substantial foreign direct investment, and has seemingly weathered recent economic turbulence better than most.

All of this has substantiated the general thrust of Bush's Enterprise for the Americas initiative set out in June 1990, whereby Central and Latin America were to 'trade not aid' their way out of the debt crisis. This message has been reaffirmed by drastic cuts in US aid programmes to the region. Between 1992 and 1995 aid was almost halved to $760 million and in 1996 Congress cut foreign aid again by one-fifth, with the loss to Latin America being disproportionately high. However, as if to demonstrate the essential continuity of American policy in the Western Hemisphere, neither Bush nor Clinton have been averse to using methods, when things were not going their way, which fit perfectly into the context of the 1823 Monroe Doctrine and the 1904 Roosevelt Corollary. The first and clearest demonstration of this came in 1989. In Panama, General Noriega clung to power regardless of US sanctions and defeat in the May national election. Deputy Secretary of State Lawrence Eagleburger warned that action would be taken against his 'illegal' government unless it were removed by 1 September. When this did not happen, the US itself duly embarked on what many see as illegal action. In October, America backed a coup to depose Noriega. It failed. On 15 December, Panama declared a state of war with the US. The Bush administration, after a car carrying American officers was shot at, launched Operation Just Cause, involving the deployment of 25,000 troops, six days of fighting, and contravention of OAS and UN charters. In justification of US actions Noriega's drug trafficking activities, democratic principles, the integrity of the Panama Canal, and defence of American citizens were all cited. Certainly, these factors played some part in the decision. More decisive, though, was that Bush was both personally embarrassed by Noriega and anxious to signal that, despite the end of the Cold War and President Carter's Canal treaty, the US was still not prepared to tolerate challenges to its predominance in the Western Hemisphere[15] (see Chapter 10).

Less dramatic but similarly instructive of US attitudes was the crisis in Haiti. In December 1990, Haiti returned Jean-Bertrand Aristide in its first-ever democratic election. Seven months later, his fragile democracy was overturned by the military, a threat faced by many fledging democracies in the Western Hemisphere. The US was swift to condemn this action but President Bush was equally swift to pursue a far less noble policy in respect of thousands of fleeing refugees. He ordered the Coast Guard to return them to Haiti. This approach was lambasted by Clinton as 'cruel' and inhumane during the 1992 election campaign. Yet, once in office, it was a policy that he, too, pursued, along with an initial failure to honour a pledge to restore Aristide to power. As time went by and a UN brokered deal in July 1993 failed, Clinton eventually decided to act, albeit not until his hand was forced by domestic political pressure from the TransAfrica organisation and the Congressional Black Caucus. In July 1994, the US persuaded the UN Security Council to approve a resolution insisting on Aristide's return. Subsequently, former President Carter led a negotiating team which, backed by a threat of invasion, secured Aristide's return to power. However, this was not done before the US had again flexed its military muscle. Even the peaceful arrival in Haiti of 20,000 US troops sent a clear message to the Western Hemisphere.

Despite shows of military strength, efforts to 'marketise and democratise', and clear US preponderance in the Americas, neither Bush nor Clinton have achieved all their goals. This is due principally to four factors. First, without a communist threat there has been less urgency to address disorder. Hence, it was left to the UN to mediate the previously vital conflict in El Salvador, which it did successfully in 1992, and Clinton took three years before visiting South America. Second, the huge economic disparities between North and South America create very different agendas. This was clear at the 1992 Earth Summit in Rio de Janeiro when the two sides talked past each other. The debt crisis preoccupied the Third World whilst concern to preserve US economic a contemporary multipolar world are greater and perhaps harder to address than the Cold War ever was.

10 Contemporary challenges

> On the eve of a new century, we have the power and the duty to build a new era of peace and security.
>
> President Clinton, State of the Union Address, 27 January 1998[1]

By the end of 1993 Clinton felt some nostalgia for the Cold War. Its demise had removed the stability of bipolarity and the easily defined strategic priorities that went with it. These had helped to structure both the Western Alliance and US policy options, including difficult decisions such as whether or not to intervene in other states. Nearly a decade after the end of the Cold War, and nine years after President Bush's announcement during the Gulf War of a New World Order, the US still strives to redefine its role amidst an international terrain that is more variegated and demands new thinking. Dramatic change has fomented the most far ranging debate about US foreign policy since the Second World War. It embraces worries about decline, hopes for democracy, and an upsurge of neo-isolationism. This latter phenomenon has been spawned by fears of foreign economic challenges to US jobs and a naive belief that a fortress America could rise above both foreign security challenges and the entanglements of complex economic interdependence. After Bush's internationalism came Clinton's more isolationist focus on domestic affairs. As the most resonant anecdote of the 1992 presidential election campaign claimed: 'it's the economy, stupid'. Despite this conviction, Clinton's preoccupation with domestic affairs gradually gave way to the demands of the foreign domain. By late 1995, he mused at one point that the longer he experienced office 'the more I become convinced that there is no longer a clear distinction between what is foreign and domestic.'[2]

Characterising US foreign policy in the 1990s and trying to set its agenda are not easy. In the previous chapter we examined how the US reacted to specific challenges in different regions. In this chapter we shall

New and not so new conceptions of the world out there

One of the most difficult problems for US foreign policy-makers since 1991 has been fundamental disagreement about the nature of the post-Cold War world. All we can show here is the spectrum range: Huntington's 'Clash of Civilisations'; Mearsheimer's 'Back to the Future' unstable world of multipolarity; Waltz's world of nuclear proliferation; the democratic triumphalism of Francis Fukuyama's 'End of History'; and Michael Doyle's argument, derived from Kantian philosophy, that democracies do not go to war with each other.[5]

Huntington's hypothesis is that 'the fundamental source of conflict in this new world will not be primarily ideological or primarily economic. The great divisions among humankind and the dominating source of conflict will be cultural.'[6] He identified eight major civilisations: Western; Confucian, Japanese; Islamic; Hindu; Slavic-Orthodox; Latin American; and possibly [!] African. He believes that conflict will occur along fault lines, especially between the West and Islam, because of differences of history, language, culture, and 'most important, religion.' Just how plausible this is depends on the credibility of Huntington's categories. Why should there be such distinctive differences between the West, Latin America, and Slavic Orthodox civilisations when Christianity is a common thread and Huntington claims religion to be the most important defining factor of civilisations? Does he exaggerate the reaction against Western values and over-emphasise the impact of religious fundamentalism? If it is so difficult for cultures to assimilate or co-exist, how is it that the American experience has been, although not without its difficulties, so successful? Are his categories really as impermeable as he suggests? Are they pitted one against the other? Do not the things that make us all part of common humanity override the cultural differences? Or are these points simply the cant of over-optimistic idealism?

In 1990, John Mearsheimer warned the world that the end of the Cold War made Europe more not less dangerous. To many this seemed absurd, but Mearsheimer and the idea of absurdity do not go easily together. He is a neo-realist who believes that first order causes of war 'lie more in the structure of the international system than in the nature of individual states.'[7] The anarchic world order means that each state has to look after itself. If one's trust in another state were betrayed then disaster might follow. 'This competitive world is peaceful when it is obvious that the costs and risks of going to war are high, and the benefits of going to war are low. Two aspects of military power are at the heart of this incentive structure: the distribution of power between states, and the nature of power available to them.'[8] The Cold War peace in Europe was thus the result of a bipolar distribution of roughly equal power based ultimately on nuclear weapons. With the disappearance of that structure the distribution of power will become multipolar and unstable because it is more complex. There are more possibilities for shifting alliances. Calculations of power are more difficult to make and there is greater scope for misunderstandings. In short, Europe has become a potentially volatile sub-system in which costs and risks of going to war are lowered and benefits of going to war enhanced. To counteract these dangers, Mearsheimer proposes that there should be a managed proliferation of nuclear weapons (at least to Germany) in order to create a system of complex deterrence, that the US should remain in Europe to help manage the system, and that it should take steps to prevent the re-emergence of hyper-nationalism.

The key problem with Mearsheimer's analysis is vagueness about the relationship between the domestic (second order) and international systemic (first order) causal factors of war. Just how important second order causes are and how the line should be drawn separating them from first order causes is never clearly stipulated. If domestic second order causes such as hyper-nationalism turned out in fact to be first order causes, as they seem to be in the Serbian-Kosovo tragedy, then in other situations democracy might be similarly elevated in the causal chain. Perhaps the picture is not quite as Mearsheimer represents it. Neo-realism needs to take account of other dimensions. One would be foolish not to take on board Mearsheimer's arguments, which punctured the naive optimism of liberal idealists at the end of the Cold War, but it might also be less than wise not to give more weight to the impact of democracy and economic interdependence on the way that the international system operates.

Kenneth Waltz, with more undiluted neo-realist assumptions about systemic explanations of international relations, arrives at a slightly more optimistic scenario than Mearsheimer. Waltz believes that nuclear weapons are the great levellers, which create equality among states because of deterrence. He looks for proliferation to sustain order and allow states to pursue economic competition. States will continue to prioritise their own selfish national interests but in a world where anarchy and competition is moderated and ordered by nuclear deterrence.[9]

The realist/neo-realist picture of the post-Cold War world is very much back-to-the-future, in that a multipolar system has re-emerged after the stability of the bipolar Cold War, but it is governed by the same basic variables of international anarchy and the need for each state to defend itself. For Mearsheimer, the problem is the inherent instability of multipolarity; for Waltz, the key is the stabilising effect of nuclear deterrence, which leads him to advocate proliferation. However, he still sees dangers in an uncertain world where security competition continues much as before. For neither is there a New World Order in the way Bush spoke of it.

Notwithstanding the force of arguments from the more pessimistic schools of thought, ideas of a democratic and multilateralist New World Order persist. For liberal democratic idealists, the systemic constraints of the realist and neo-realist models – the struggle for survival under anarchy when constantly confronted with the security dilemma and when nation state, or communitarian values, always override cosmopolitan or universal values – do not necessarily prevail. For those, like Fukuyama, such constraints have been transcended with the demise of ideological dialectics and its result: 'the end of history'. There is now the potential to spread democracy and the free market throughout the world. According to Michael Doyle this is likely to bring peace because democracies in their respect for individuals exercise restraint and have peaceful intentions in their foreign policies. For many this is the primary mission of the US. In 1994, an article in *Foreign Affairs* lamented Clinton's failure to pursue this agenda vigorously.

> Much suffering could be spared if the United States, working with other countries through multilateral institutions like the United Nations, the Organization of American States ..., or NATO, took a clear position on what is not tolerable in world affairs and then moved decisively to enforce the collective will in areas where such efforts could produce results. A historical opportunity to give structure and meaning to the post-Cold War world is being missed and will be ever more difficult to recover later.[10]

This agenda operates from a number of assumptions which both beg important questions at the heart of an on-going debate between cosmopolitan and communitarian theorists and which always tends to identify the position of the US with the collective or universal good. These ideas are ubiquitous in the rhetoric and policy statements of the US. In *Pax Democratica*, James R. Huntley, with the approbation of ex-Secretary of State, Lawrence Eagleburger, articulated these views in terms of proposals for an alliance of democracies that should work together to foster economic and security communities that could act multilaterally to promote an enlarging peaceful democratic community. But, it would be one that would have to intervene to police non-democratic states. In considering how a democratic security community might do this, Huntley stumbles against the persistent realist obstacle to multilateralism.

At least initially, the United States probably would not accept a situation in which it could be committed to war against its will; the voting must be carefully calculated. On the other hand, it should not be possible for Luxembourg, or Portugal, or even France or Britain alone, to immobilize the Alliance in the face of a preponderant majority.[11]

It seems rather anomalous that in this idealistic game respect for *force majeure* could trump what is right (assuming that the US is not infallible) and there should be one rule for the strongest and another for all the rest. In fact, this new idealism is premised on three shaky foundations: first, that there are no alternatives to Western liberal democracy worthy of serious consideration; second, that democracies do not go to war with each other; and third, that under US leadership there will be a growth of multilateral actions. The first assumption exhibits a closed mind that seems alien to the very tradition of thought that has spawned it. The second ignores the criticisms of theorists such as Mearsheimer, and, even if it were true that democracies do not go to war with each other, there would still be the problem of their relations with other non-democratic states. And the third assumption has not only the serious defect identified and then glossed over by Huntley, but also a series of *de facto* problems. They consist of US rejection of assertive multilateralism in Presidential Directive 25, 5 May 1994, after the UN *debacle* in Somalia; its lack of effective action on global warming; reluctance to pay UN dues; and:

> American reservations surfaced during [1997] in negotiations to ban anti-personnel mines, to prohibit the use of child soldiers, and to establish an international criminal court. In each case, Washington paid lip service to the proposal while U.S. negotiators worked hard to weaken it. Because of these reservations, the international community has shown a new willingness to bypass the United States in strengthening human rights law.[12]

The conclusion to be drawn from all this is that on the one hand, in practice, the US does not live up to its own professed ideals. From this perspective it looks to outsiders as if the US is manipulating the language of idealism to further its own interests, and its purpose is thus no different from that which uses traditional forms of power for achieving security in an anarchical world order. On the other hand, rhetoric suggests that realism and idealism are reconciled by the implicit claim that US ideals are universally valid – engagement and democratic enlargement and promotion of the free market – and by the implicit assumption that the US has the power to realise this New World Order – 'a historical opportunity to give structure and meaning to the post-Cold War world.' This attitude not only dismisses the cosmopolitan and communitarian debate too lightly, it also raises important practical questions as it fuels the desire for US intervention abroad.

Security and interventionism

'But She Goes Not Abroad In Search Of Monsters to Destroy'
John Quincy Adams 1821

How, when, why and at what cost should the US intervene militarily in the affairs of other states and how should exit strategies be formulated? These questions were and are difficult to answer because of the ongoing debate about the nature of the new international system, because of the merging of domestic and foreign policy, and because of uncertainty about the nature of a relevant security agenda.

The end of the Cold War accelerated a trend to see the concept of security in a different light. Liberated from the constraints of bipolarity, which had been bedrocked, in security terms, on the respective nuclear deterrents of the two superpowers, less traditional notions of security began to gain currency. All of a sudden, security studies were able to consider more broadly cast definitions that had previously been pushed to the periphery or totally excluded from consideration by the imperative of survival in a nuclear perilous world. According to scholars such as Barry Buzan in his widely read *People, States and Fear*[13], there was need for radical change which would incorporate crime, drugs, health, economics, and identity among other factors into the study of security communities. Their emergence does not entail the abandonment of the nation state as an actor, but the state now has to be seen in the context of these more important players. Such ideas further complicated conceptions of the international terrain, especially when other scholars, such as David Baldwin and Lawrence Freedman, in turn challenged the new security studies, alleging that they were conceptually confused and ill-focused. These are exactly the same kind of criticisms that the authors of the new security studies had levelled at the traditionalists.[14]

US policy-makers responded to all this by establishing three priorities: emphasis on the importance of engagement and democratic enlargement as expressed by NSA Anthony Lake in September 1993; the promotion of the free market; and concern about regional security problems, which incorporated some of the new security thinking. US intervention in Panama in 1989 provided a benchmark for the new policy and its criteria for, and aims of, intervention.

The re-orientation of US foreign policy to regional conflicts was directed by Bush and his Chairman of the Joint Chiefs of Staff, General Colin Powell. The key question was: Under what circumstances should the US intervene? This was not a new question. Defence Secretary Caspar Weinberger promulgated his answer under Cold War conditions in November 1984.

1   Our vital interests must be at stake.

2   The issues are so important for the future of the United States and our allies that we are prepared to commit enough forces to win.

3   We have clearly defined political and military objectives, which we must secure.

4   We have sized our forces to meet our objectives.

5   We have some reasonable assurance of the support of the American people.

6   U.S. forces are committed to combat only as a last resort.[15]

The new strategy envisaged by Bush and Powell built on the Weinberger Doctrine.

> When a "fire" starts that might require committing armed forces, we need to evaluate the circumstances. Relevant questions include: Is the political objective we seek to achieve important, clearly defined and understood? Have all other nonviolent policy means failed? Will military force achieve the objective? At what cost? Have the gains and risks been analyzed? How might the situation that we seek to alter, once it is altered by force, develop further and what might be the consequences?[16]

At the end of Bush's presidency, Powell recorded a litany of successful US missions and claimed the reason 'for our success is that in every instance we have carefully matched the use of military force to our political objectives.'[17] But just how accurately does this sum up the US experience during these crucial hinge years of the closing of the Cold War and the opening onto a New World Order? To what extent did the Panama operation fit the new template?

As we saw in Chapter 9, the problem was General Manuel Noriega, a one-time recruit of the CIA when Bush had been Director in the 1970s. Noriega in the late 1980s was now no friend of the US. He voided the May 1989 Panama elections and remained stubbornly in power. In the key decision-making discussions about what the US should do, 'George Bush sat like a patron on a bar stool coolly observing a brawl while his advisers went hard at it.'[18] NSA Brent Scowcroft wanted to know possible casualty numbers and what would happen if Noriega escaped. No one could answer. But it was anticipated that a lot of 'real estate would get chewed up' and that there would be 'chaos' in the early stages. In other words, there was no guarantee that if American forces went in that they would be able to control the situation.

> The key issue remained whether we had sufficient provocation to act. We had reasons – Noriega's contempt for democracy, his drug trafficking and indictment, the death of the American Marine, the threat to our treaty rights to the canal with this unreliable figure ruling Panama. And, unspoken, there was George Bush's personal antipathy to Noriega, a third-rate dictator thumbing his nose at the United States. I shared that distaste. … The questions continued thick and fast, until it started to look as if we were drifting away from the decision at hand … But then Bush, after everyone had had his say, gripped the arms of his chair and rose. "Okay, let's do it," he said. "The hell with it."[19]

So much for careful and objective application of the rules of engagement! Old-fashioned hegemony over the Western Hemisphere and the long US tradition of unilateral military action there tell us more about the invasion of Panama than the new security agenda, the rules of engagement for regional security crises, democratic enlargement and the desirability of multilateral operations. But then is this really surprising because for all his talk of a New World Order, Bush remained stubbornly conservative and cautiously realist in his foreign policy-making. Even in the Gulf War, which seemed to promise much for the future because of Soviet involvement in multilateral co-operation, matters could be explained in traditional realist terms. For example, the dominant considerations according to some were US national interests in oil supplies and the need to get others to pay for the military operation because of continuing fears about US decline. Furthermore, while Powell and others later held up the Gulf War as a prime example of how to intervene in a regional crisis, one of the cardinal rules of engagement was not applied. An exit strategy was not fully worked out. Nearly ten years on, substantial US military forces still police the area and seek to ensure the success of the UN mission concerning the abolition of Iraq's weapons of mass destruction.

Thus, despite the rhetoric, there remained uncertainty about the way the international system had changed and considerable ambiguity about both an appropriate style of US foreign policy and engagement criteria for regional crises. For a while, the Clinton administration looked set to disperse these ambiguities and come out and commit the US more fully and actively to democratic enlargement, humanitarian causes, human rights, and multilateralism through the media of organisations such as the UN, NATO and the OAS. However, promulgating Wilsonian liberal ideology is one thing, responsibility and actions are different.

In the 1992 election campaign, Clinton had been critical of Bush and had spoken out in favour of a more positive policy on Bosnia. However, it took a long time and many deaths in Bosnia before Clinton made action match rhetoric. In his first year in office he concentrated on domestic affairs and even when, in 1993, he and his advisers affirmed that the US must remain internationalist, it was unclear how this would be translated into action. While Secretary of State Christopher gave a forceful exposition of the Doyle democratic peace theory,[20] Somalia undermined faith in assertive multilateralism. It seemed that the US would have to take the lead because NATO exercised power more effectively than the UN and NATO only worked well if the US was at its head. This, in turn, again raised the question about when, where, and how the US should intervene.

Bosnia soon provided a test case for this more cautious pragmatism. Until 1995, the US maintained a distance between itself and the crisis there. Clinton averred that there were no US interests directly involved and public opinion did not mandate a more vigorous line. Nevertheless, while both rhetoric and policy prevaricated, the Bottom-up Review of military strategy initiated by the President was released in September 1993 and appeared to confirm the internationalist and Wilsonian idealist facet of Clinton. Apart from predictable conclusions, such as the need to restrict the spread of nuclear weapons, the emphasis was on regional conflicts. The US needed the ability to deal with two major ones simultaneously. In addition, it should seek to foster democratic values and be prepared to 'participate effectively in multilateral peace enforcement and unilateral intervention operations that could include peacekeeping, humanitarian assistance, counterdrug and counterterrorism activities.'[21] So, regional intervention policy was still the main focus with a stronger commitment than Bush's to democratic enlargement. Was it for these reasons that US policy in Bosnia was transformed in 1995 with the launching of the Holbrooke mission which led to the Dayton Peace Accords, the commitment of 20,000 US troops, and the on-going US military presence there? Not according to one scholar.

> The State Department's Bosnia study confirms that most senior foreign policy officials, most notably the president himself, were surprised to learn in June 1995 that U.S. troops might soon be on their

Conclusion

So what does the future hold? A clash of civilisations, or an on-going competition for security and power much as in the past? Or, will there be a more peaceful world where the spread of democracy, the UN, economic interdependence and a growing awareness of the things that threaten all humankind bond the states that make up the world into a more collective enterprise for the good of all? One suspects that there will be elements at work from all of these alternatives, but whatever way it turns out, the future will depend much upon the women and men who run the foreign policy of the US. How they understand the world, cope with, and direct it will help determine the future for us all. Realist appreciation of problems that they will confront in dealing with states concerned with power and security in a system where anarchy is still an important characteristic must be a part of their understanding. But the effects of the growth of democracy, economic interdependence and non-state actors (including regional blocs such as NAFTA and the EU) and the idealist imagination, not bounded solely by Western values, have all got parts to play as well. Fukuyama's vision, of the monolithic triumph of the West, is a rank impoverishment of the richness of this world.

There are two vitally important issues for the future of US foreign policy. The first is to maintain the integrity of its constitutional democracy. The second is to ensure that when Americans are asked to lay their lives on the line for foreign policy goals that this is properly justified, because a violent and premature death is the untimely snatching away of that most precious of all rights – the right to life. These two issues are not separable, even though they seem to refer to the domestic and the foreign spheres. The imperial presidency demonstrated just how interconnected they are. US policy-makers need to understand complexity, value democratic controls and accountability, recognise worth in others, realise power is more than brute force, and have imagination to pursue a better world order through accommodation with others without endangering the security of the US. These are not easily acquired qualities, but they are prerequisites if the US is to develop a democratic and effective foreign policy capable of meeting the challenges of the future.

Notes

1 US foreign policy

1 M. Albright, 'The Testing of American Foreign Policy', *Foreign Affairs*, 77(6), 1998, pp. 50–64.
2 For further reading on the nature of foreign policy and its challenges for the US see: Hans J. Morgenthau, *Politics Among Nations : The Struggle for Power and Peace*, New York, Knopf, 1985, 6th ed. revised by Kenneth Thompson; Graham T. Allison, *Essence of Decision: Explaining the Cuban Missile Crisis,* Boston, Little Brown, 1971; Laura Neack, Jeanne A.K. Hay & Patrick J. Haney (eds.), *Foreign Policy Analysis: Continuity and Change in Its Second Generation*, Englewood Cliffs, New Jersey, Prentice Hall, 1995; Susan Strange, 'Political Economy and International Relations', in Ken Booth & Steve Smith, *International Relations Theory Today*, Cambridge, Polity Press, 1995; Miroslav Nincic, *Democracy and Foreign Policy: the Fallacy of Political Realism,* New York, Columbia University Press, 1992.
3 H.S. Commager, *Living Ideas in America*, New York, Harper, 1951, pp. 143–7, Washington's Farewell Address.
4 There is further discussion of democratic peace theory in chapter 10: see also Michael W. Doyle, 'Kant, Liberal Legacies and Foreign Affairs' Parts 1 & 2, *Philosophy and Public Affairs,* 12, 1983, pp. 205–35 & 323–53.
5 Hans. J. Morgenthau, *A New Foreign Policy for the United States*, London, Pall Mall Press, 1969; also, see chapter 7.
6 Alan P. Dobson (ed.), with S. Malik & G. Evans (assistant eds.), *Deconstructing and Reconstructing the Cold War,* Andover, Ashgate, 1999.
7 Hereafter the Nationalist Chinese island is referred to as Taiwan.
8 Arthur M. Schlesinger Jr., *The Imperial Presidency*, New York, Popular Library, 1974.

2 The US and the Cold War

1 For many years the Cold War was seen very much as an exclusive US–Soviet affair. Literature from the late 1970s onwards has shown the fallacy of that. Alan Bullock, *Ernest Bevin: Foreign Secretary*, Oxford, OUP, 1985; Anne Deighton, *The Impossible Peace: Britain, the Division of Germany and the Origins of the Cold War,* Oxford, Clarendon,

1990; Charles S. Maier (ed.), *The Cold War in Europe: Era of a Divided Continent*, Princeton, Marcus Wiener, 1996.

2   George F. Kennan, 'X', 'The Sources of Soviet Conduct', *Foreign Affairs*, 25, 1947, pp. 566–82.

3   Cited by E.R. May, *American Cold War Strategy: Interpreting NSC 68*, New York, Bedford Books, 1993, p. 9.

4   *Foreign Relations of the United States* 1950, vol.1, NSC-68, 14 Apr. 1950, pp. 243–44.

5   J.L. Gaddis, *Strategies of Containment*, Oxford, Oxford University Press, 1982, p. 95.

6   Ibid., p. 151, source James Shepley, 'How Dulles Averted War', *Life Magazine*, 40, 16 Jan. 1956.

3   Superpower collaboration and confrontation

1   W.W. Rostow, *The Stages of Economic Growth: A Non-Communist Manifesto*, Cambridge, Cambridge University Press, 1962.

2   For more on Kennedy see M.R. Beschloss, *The Crisis Years: Kennedy and Krushchev, 1960–63*, New York, Edward Burlingame Books, 1991; A.M. Schlesinger Jr., *A Thousand Days: John F. Kennedy in the White House*, Boston, Houghton Mifflin, 1965; T.G. Paterson (ed.), *Kennedy's Quest for Victory: American Foreign Policy, 1961–1963*, New York, Oxford University Press, 1989.

3   J. Spanier, *American Foreign Policy Since World War II*, New York, Holt, Rinehart, & Winston, 1985, p.168.

4   H. Kissinger, *American Foreign Policy*, New York, W.W. Norton, 1977, p. 305. For more about Kissinger's *realpolitik* approach and the policy of *détente* R. Garthoff, *Détente and Confrontation: American–Soviet Relations from Nixon to Reagan*, Washington, The Brookings Institute, 1994; W. Isaacson, *Kissinger: A Biography*, New York, Simon and Schuster, 1992.

5   For the change in US policy toward China see I.J. Kim, *The Strategic Triangle: China, the United States and the Soviet Union*, New York, Paragon House, 1987; H. Harding, *A Fragile Relationship: The United States and China Since 1972*, Washington D.C., Brookings Institute, 1992.

6   It has been argued that the US never had at its disposal the incentives and sanctions that were necessary to moderate Soviet behaviour. R.S. Litwak, *Détente and the Nixon Doctrine: American Foreign Policy and the Pursuit of Stability, 1969–1976*, Cambridge, Cambridge University Press, 1984, p. 93.

7   For discussion of Carter's dilemmas see G. Smith, *Morality, Reason and Power: American Diplomacy in the Carter Years*, New York, Hill and Wang, 1986; L. Schoultz, *Human Rights and the United States Policy Towards Latin America*, Princeton N.J., Princeton, 1981; J. Muravchik, *The Uncertain Crusade: Jimmy Carter and the Dilemmas of Human Rights Policy*, London, Hamilton Press, 1986.

8   J.L. Gaddis, *The United States and the End of the Cold War: Implications, Reconsiderations, Provocations*, New York, Oxford University Press, 1992, p. 123.

9   J. Dumbrell, *American Foreign Policy: Carter to Clinton*, London, Macmillan Press, 1997, p. 74.

10   *Ibid.*, p. 87.

11   Gaddis, *The United States and the end of the Cold War*, p. 131.

12   For more on the Reagan approach to containment see D. Mervin, *Ronald Reagan and the American Presidency*, London, Longman, 1990; R.A. Dallek, *Ronald Reagan: The Politics of Symbolism*, Cambridge, Harvard University Press, 1984; R.J. McMahaon,

'Making Sense of American Foreign Policy During the Reagan Years', *Diplomatic History*, 1995, vol. 19, pp. 367–84.

13 Cited by S.J. Ball, *The Cold War*, p. 228.

14 R.A. Melanson, *American Foreign Policy Since the Vietnam War: The Search for Consensus from Nixon to Clinton*, 2nd edit. New York, M.E. Sharpe, 1996, p.213.

15 So-called because it involved East and West Germany plus France, Britain, the US, and the Soviet Union.

16 For more on Bush see especially M.R. Beschloss & S. Talbott, *At the Highest Levels: The Inside Story of the End of the Cold War*, Boston, Little, Brown, 1993.

4 Economic statecraft

1 David Horowitz, *Free World Colossus,* (New York, Hill & Wang, 1971); Immanuel Wallerstein, *The Modern World System, 2 Vols.* (Academic Press, New York, 1974); Paul Kennedy, *The Rise and Fall of the Great Powers,* New York, Random House, 1987; Joseph Nye, *Bound to Lead: The Changing Nature of American Power,* New York, Basic Books, 1990; Stephen Gill, *American Hegemony and the Trilateral Commission,* Cambridge, CUP, 1990; Susan Strange, 'The Persistent Myth of Lost Hegemony', *International Organization,* 41(4), 1987, pp. 551–74.

2 It was succeeded in 1967 by the European Community (EC), and in 1993 by the European Union (EU).

3 Harry Magdoff, *The Age of Imperialism: The Economics of US Foreign Policy*, New York, Modern Reader Paperbacks, 1969. Magdoff was one of many in the New Left historical school which included luminaries such as William Appleman Williams, Gabriel Kolko, Gar Alperovitz, Lloyd Gardner, Diane Shaver Clemens and a host of others.

4 United States Information Service: text State of the Union Message, 19 Jan. 1999.

5 The US and Europe, 1950–89

1 C.S. Maier, 'Alliance and Autonomy: European Identity and U.S. Foreign Policy Objectives in the Truman Years', M.J. Lacey (ed.), *The Truman Presidency,* Cambridge, Cambridge University Press, 1989, pp. 273–98; G. Lundestad, *"Empire" by Integration: the United States and European Integration, 1945–1997*, Oxford, Oxford University Press, 1998, pp. 1–5.

2 For the Berlin Crisis see H.M. Catudal, *Kennedy and the Berlin Wall Crisis: A Case Study in US Decision Making,* Berlin, Berlin Verlag, 1980; J.C. Ausland, *Kennedy, Khrushchev, and the Berlin–Cuba Crisis, 1961–64*, Oslo, Scandanavia, 1996; J.S. Gearson, *Harold Macmillan and the Berlin Wall Crisis 1958–1962: The Limits of Interest and Force*, Basingstoke, Macmillan, 1998; J.M. Schick, *The Berlin Crisis, 1958–1962*, Philadelphia, University of Philadelphia Press, 1971.

3 For details of the EDC-Indo-China connection see J. Aimaq, *For Europe or for Empire? French Colonial Ambitions and the European Army Plan*, Lund, Sweden, Lund University Press, 1996. For the Anglo-American relationship see A.P. Dobson, *Anglo-American Relations in the Twentieth Century*, London, Routledge, 1995.

4 M. Hogan, *The Marshall Plan: America, Britain, and the Reconstruction of Western Europe, 1947–52,* Cambridge, Cambridge University Press, 1987, p. 445.

5 E. Dell, *The Schuman Plan and the Abdication of British Leadership in Europe,* Oxford, Oxford University Press, 1995; C. Lord, *Absent at the Creation: Britain and the Formation of the European Community*, Aldershot, Dartmouth, 1996.

6 For the EDC controversy and West German rearmament see E. Fursdon, *The European*

Defence Community: A History, London, Macmillan, 1980; S. Dockrill, *Britain's Policy for West German Rearmament, 1950–1955,* Cambridge, Cambridge University Press, 1991.

7   Kennedy cited by G. Lundestad, *Empire by Integration,* p. 68.

8   For MLF see P. Winand, *Eisenhower, Kennedy, and the United States of Europe,* London, Macmillan, 1997, especially pp. 203–45 & pp. 317–56. For rejection of Britain's EEC application W. Kaiser, 'The Bomb and Europe: Britain, France, and the EEC Negotiations 1961–63', *Journal of European Integration History,* 1995, vol. 1, pp. 65–85; R. Steininger, 'Great Britain's First EEC Failure in January 1963', *Diplomacy and Statecraft,* vol. 7, 1996, pp. 404–35. For the trade dispute, R.B. Talbot, *The Chicken War,* Ames, Iowa State University, 1978.

9   R.L. Rubenstein (ed.), *The Dissolving Alliance: The United States and the Future of Europe,* New York, Paragon House, 1987; J. Joffe, *The Limited Partnership: Europe, the United States, and the Burdens of Alliance,* Cambridge Mass., Ballinger, 1987; M. Smith, *Western Europe and the United States: The Uncertain Alliance,* London, Allen & Unwin, 1984.

10   W. Goldstein (ed.), *Reagan's Leadership and the Atlantic Alliance: Views From Europe and America,* London, Pergammon-Brassey, 1986; S. Gill (ed.), *Atlantic Relations: Beyond the Reagan Era,* New York, St. Martin's Press, 1989; K. Featherstone & R. Ginsberg, *The United States and the European Union in the 1990s: Partners in Transition,* London, Macmillan, 1996; G. Lundestad, 'The United States and Western Europe Under Reagan', in D.E. Kyvig, *Reagan and the World,* New York, Greenwood, 1990, pp. 39–66.

11   A.P. Dobson, 'Aspects of Anglo-American Aviation Diplomacy 1976–93', *Diplomacy and Statecraft,* 1993, vol.4, pp. 235–55.

12   K. Schwabe, 'The United States and European Integration: 1947–1957', in C. Wurm (ed.), *Western Europe and Germany: The Beginnings of European Integration 1945– 1960,* Oxford, Berg, 1995, p. 129; R.T. Griffiths, 'The European Historical Experience', in K. Middlemas (ed.), *Orchestrating Europe: The Informal Politics of European Union 1973–1995,* London, Fontana Press, 1995, pp. 1–70; A.P. Dobson, 'The USA, Britain, and the Question of Hegemony', in G. Lundestad (ed.), *No End to Alliance. The United States and Western Europe: Past, Present and Future,* London, Macmillan Press, 1998, pp. 134–166.

13   West Germany, France, Belgium, Netherlands, Luxembourg, Italy, Britain, Denmark, Ireland, Greece, Spain, and Portugal.

6   Hegemony and the Western Hemisphere

1   For good examples of this kind of literature see: Thomas J. McCormick, *America's Half Century: United States Foreign Policy in the Cold War,* Baltimore, John Hopkins UP, 1989; David P. Calleo, *Beyond American Hegemony: The Future of the Western Alliance,* New York, Basic Books, 1987; Arthur A. Stein, 'The Hegemon's Dilemma: Great Britain, the United States, and the International Economic Order', *International Organization,* 38(2), 1984, pp. 355–86.

2   William Appleman Williams, *The Tragedy of American Diplomacy,* New York, Dell, 1962.

3   G.T. Allison, *Essence of Decision: Explaining the Cuban Missile Crisis,* Boston, Little Brown, 1971; R.A. Divine (ed.), *The Cuban Missile Crisis,* New York, Marcus Wiener, 1988; J.L. Gaddis, *We Now Know: Rethinking Cold War History,* Oxford, Clarendon,

1997, ch. 9; L.V. Scott, *Macmillan, Kennedy and the Cuban Missile Crisis: Political, Military and Intelligence Aspects*, Basingstoke, Macmillan, 1999.

4   There is a burgeoning literature on crisis management which was given much impetus by Allison's, *Essence of Decision*, but students should compare the basis for his admiration of the way Kennedy handled the crisis with what Gaddis has to say in *We Now Know*, ch. 9. For an introduction to crisis decsion-making see Paul R. Viotti and Mark V. Kauppi, *International Relations Theory: Realism, Pluralism, Globalism, and Beyond*, Boston, Allyn and Bacon, 1999, ch. 3.

7   The US and Asia, 1945–89

1   For Korea see M. Hastings, *The Korean War*, London, Michael Joseph, 1987; R.J. Foot, *The Wrong War: American Policy and Dimensions of the Korean Conflict*, Ithaca, N.Y., Cornell University Press, 1985; B. Cumings, *The Origins of the Korean War, Vol. 2, The Roaring of the Cataract*, Princeton, Princeton University Press, 1992.

2   D.F. Fleming, *The Cold War and its Origins, 1917–1960*, 2 vols., London, Allen & Unwin, 1961, pp. 1067–68.

3   For evidence of Stalin's encouragement of North Korea see D. Heinzig, 'Stalin, Mao, Kim and Korean War Origins, 1950: A Documentary Discrepancy', *The Cold War International History Project Bulletin*, (1996/97), Issues 8–9, pp. 240–43; S. Goncharov, J.W. Lewis, X. Litai, *Uncertain Partners: Stalin, Mao, and the Korean War*, Stanford, Stanford University Press, 1993, pp. 143–45; J.l. Gaddis, *We Now Know*, pp. 70–75.

4   D. Horowitz, *The Free World Colossus*, New York, Hill & Wang, 1971, p. 119.

5   Literature on Vietnam is enormous riven by debate about the justification of US actions and why its intervention was unsuccessful. Amongst the best accounts is G.C. Herring, *America's Longest War: The United States and Vietnam 1950–1975*, New York, Wiley, 1979. For a clash over the morality of US actions see T. Taylor, *Nuremberg and Vietnam: An American Tragedy*, Chicago, Quadrangle Books, 1970; G. Lewy, *America in Vietnam: Illusion, Myth, and Reality*, New York, Oxford University Press, 1978. For the 'winnability' debate see B. Palmer Jr., *The 25 Year War: America's Military Role in Vietnam*, Lexington Ky, Kentucky University Press, 1984; G. Kahin, *Intervention: How America Became Involved in Vietnam*, New York, Knopf, 1986.

6   For more on US–Japanese relations see W. LaFeber, *The Clash: A History of US–Japanese Relations*, New York, W.W. Norton, 1997; M. Schaller, *Altered States: The United States and Japan Since the Occupation*, New York, Oxford University Press, 1997; W.I. Cohen, *The United States and Japan in the Post War World*, Lexington Ky, University Press of Kentucky, 1989; W.S. Borden, *The Pacific Alliance: United States Foreign Economic Policy and Japanese Trade Recovery, 1947–1955*, Madison, University of Wisconsin Press, 1984; A. Iriye, *Across the Pacific: An Inner History of American–East Asian Relations*, New York, Harcourt, Brace, & Brace, 1967.

7   For more on US–China relations see G. Chang, *Friends and Enemies: The United States, China, and the Soviet Union, 1948–1972*, Stanford, Stanford University Press, 1990; G.A. James, *The China Connection: US Policy and the Peoples Republic of China*, Stanford, Stanford University Press, 1986; A.X. Jiang, *The United States and China*, Chicago, Chicago University Press, 1988; J.G. Stoessinger, *Nations at Dawn: China, the United States, and the Soviet Union*, 6th edit, New York, McGraw Hill, 1994.

8   For details see R.W. Meyers, *A Unique Relationship: The United States and the Republic of China under the Taiwan Relations Act*, Stanford, Stanford University Press, 1989.

8   The US, Africa and the Middle East, 1945–89

1   For further information on the US and Africa see P. Duuignan and L.H. Gann, *The United States and Africa: A History*, New York, Cambridge University Press, 1984; R.G. Patman, *The Soviet Union in the Horn of Africa: The Diplomacy of Intervention and Disengagement*, Cambridge, Cambridge University Press, 1990; M. Kalb, *Congo Cables: The Cold War in Africa from Eisenhower to Kennedy*, New York, Macmillan, 1982.

2   For more on the US and South Africa see T.J. Noer, *Cold War and Black Liberation: The United States and White Rule in Africa, 1948–68*, Columbia, Mo., University of Missouri Press, 1985; R.C. Coker, *The United States and South Africa 1968–85: Constructive Engagement and its Critics*, Durham North Carolina, Duke Press, 1986; R.K. Massie, *Loosing the Bonds: The United States and South Africa During the Apartheid Years*, New York, 1997; T. Borstelmann, *Apartheid's Reluctant Uncle: The United States and Southern Africa in the Early Cold War*, Oxford, Oxford University Press, 1993.

3   P.J. Schraeder, *United States Foreign Policy Toward Africa: Incrementalism, Crisis and Change*, Cambridge, Cambridge University Press, 1994, p. 157.

4   Eisenhower cited by W. Stivers, *America's Confrontation with Revolutionary Change in the Middle East, 1948–83*, London, Macmillan, 1986, p. 12.

5   S. Marsh, *The Anglo-American Special Relationship and the Anglo-Iranian Oil Crisis*, [PhD Thesis, 1999, publication forthcoming].

6   For details see R. Ovendale, *Britain, the United States, and the End of the Political Mandate*, Woodbridge, Royal Historical Society, 1989; R. Ovendale, *Origins of the Arab Israeli Wars*, London, Longman, 1984.

7   S. Marsh, 'The Special Relationship and the Anglo-Iranian Oil Crisis, 1950–54', *Review of International Studies*, 1998, vol. 24, pp. 529–44; S. Marsh, 'The Limits of US Cold War Hegemony', in A.P. Dobson (ed.), *Deconstructing and Reconstructing the Cold War*, pp. 89–110.

8   ARAMCO was the jointly owned subsidiary of the US oil companies Socal, Standard Oil (New Jersey), Socony and the Texas Oil Company. In order to encourage foreign investment of American capital, American tax laws were modified in 1918 to remove the threat of double taxation by allowing taxes paid abroad to be written off against US obligations. Oil deals, such as ARAMCO's in 1950, became an ingenious way of both subsidising Middle Eastern governments without congressional approval and of advantaging US companies over their rivals. For details see I. H. Anderson, *ARAMCO, The United States, and Saudi Arabia. A Study of the Dynamics of Foreign Oil Policy 1933–50*, Princeton, Princeton University Press, 1981, p. 143.

9   For details of the hostage crisis and the turbulent US–Iranian relationship, see J.A. Bill, *The Eagle and the Lion: The Tragedy of American–Iranian Relations*, New Haven, Yale University Press, 1988; G. Sick, *All Fall Down: America's Tragic Encounter With Iran*, New York, Random House, 1985.

10 See H. Kissinger, *White House Years,* London, Michael Joseph, 1979; H. Kissinger, *Years of Upheaval,* Boston, Little, Brown and Company, 1982; H. Isaacson, *Kissinger: A Biography.*

11 For details see J. Carter, *Keeping Faith: Memoirs of a President,* New York, Bantam Books, 1982; W. Quandt, *Camp David: Peacemaking and Politics,* Washington, The Brookings Institute, 1986.

12 For more on US policy toward the Middle East see B.I. Kaufman, *The Arab Middle East and the United States: Inter-Arab Rivalry and Super-Power Diplomacy,* New York, Twayne, 1996; S.L. Spiegel, *The Other Arab–Israeli Conflict: Making America's Middle East Policy from Truman to Reagan,* Chicago, University of Chicago Press, 1985; H.W.

Brands, *Into the Labyrinth: The United States and the Middle East, 1945–1993*, New York, McGraw Hill, 1994.

9   The US and the post-Cold War disorder

1   J. Mearsheimer, 'Back to the Future: Instability in Europe After the Cold War', *International Security*, 1990, vol. 15, pp. 5–57. There is a large literature on the end of the Cold War, but useful starting points are M.J. Hogan (ed.), *The End of the Cold War: Its Meanings and Implications*, Ohio State University, Cambridge University Press, 1994; Gaddis, *The United States and the End of the Cold War*; R. Garthoff, *The Great Transition: American–Soviet Relations and the End of the Cold War*, Washington, The Brookings Institute, 1994.

2   Assistance with economic recovery given initially to Poland and Hungary.

3   James Dobbins was US Deputy Assistant Secretary of State for European Affairs.

4   S. Hoffmann, 'The United States and Europe', in R.J. Lieber (ed.), *Eagle Adrift: American Foreign Policy at the End of the Century,* New York, Longman, 1997, p. 190.

5   Chapter 10 gives more detail on US policy in the Balkans. In addition, for ongoing problems see I.H. Daalder & M.G.B. Froman, 'Dayton's Incomplete Peace', *Foreign Affairs,* 1999, vol. 78, pp.106–114, E. Roberts, 'Montenegro: Trouble Ahead', *World Today,* 1999, vol. 55, pp.11–14; *International Documents and Analysis. Vol. 1: The Crisis in Kosovo,* 1989–1999, University of Cambridge, Centre of International Studies, 1999; J. Solana, 'NATO's Success in Kosovo', *Foreign Affairs,* 1999, vol. 78, pp. 114–120.

6   M. Cox, *US Foreign Policy After the Cold War: Superpower without a Mission?,* London, Pinter, 1995, p. 56.

7   J. Rosener, 'Assistance to the Former Soviet States', in J.M. Scott (ed.), *After The End: Making U.S. Foreign Policy in the post-Cold War World*, Durham: Duke University Press, 1998, pp. 225–250.

8   S. Sestanovich, 'Why the United States has no Russia Policy', in R.J. Lieber (ed.), *Eagle Adrift: American Foreign Policy at the End of the Century*, p 164.

9   G. Evans, 'Asia Pacific in the Twenty-First Century: Conflict or Cooperation?', *World Today,* 1996, vol. 52, p. 52.

10   K. Fukushima, 'The Revival of "Big Politics" in Japan', *International Affairs,* 1996, vol. 72, p. 65.

11   J. Bhagwati, 'The US–Japan Car Dispute: a Monumental Mistake', *International Affairs,* 1996, vol. 72, p. 261.

12   J.T. Rourke and R. Clark, 'Making U.S. Foreign Policy toward China in the Clinton Administration', in J.M Scott (ed.), *After The End*, p. 201.

13   P.J. Schraeder*, United States Foreign Policy Toward Africa: Incrementalism, Crisis and Change*, p. 250.

14   M. Indyk quoted by J.A. Phillips, 'Rethinking U.S. Policy in the Middle East', in A.Z. Rubinstein (ed.), *America's National Interest in a Post-Cold War World*, New York, McGraw-Hill, 1994, p. 222.

15   For further details see J. Dumbrell, *American Foreign Policy: Carter to Clinton*, pp. 132–134.

16   J.E. Rielly, 'Americans and the World: A Survey at Century's End', *Foreign Policy*, 1999, vol. 114, p. 99.

17   C.F. Bergsten, 'America and Europe: Clash of the Titans?', *Foreign Affairs,* 1999, vol. 78, p. 22.

10　Contemporary challenges

1　United States Information Agency, text Clinton's State of the Union Address, 27 Jan. 1998.
2　Ralph G. Carter, 'Congress and Post-Cold War U.S. Foreign Policy', in Scott (ed.), *After the End*, pp. 129–30.
3　Paul Kennedy, *The Rise and Fall of the Great Powers*, London, Fontana, Harper Collins, 1989, p. 666.
4　Joseph S. Nye, 'Understating US Strength', *Foreign Policy*, 1988, 72; and *Bound to Lead*. Susan Strange and Stephen Gill have respectively argued that a US, and a capitalist hegemony centred mainly in the US, continue to grow: 'The Persistent Myth of Lost Hegemony', *International Organization*, 1987, 41(4), pp. 551–74; *American Hegemony and the Trilateral Commission*, Cambridge, Cambridge University Press, 1990.
5　Samuel P. Huntington, 'The Clash of Civilizations', *Foreign Affairs*, 1993, 72, pp. 22–49; Mearsheimer, *Back to the Future*; Kenneth Waltz, 'The Emerging Structure of International Politics', *International Security*, 1993, 18, pp. 44–79; Francis Fukuyama, *The End of History and the Last Man*, London, Hamish Hamilton, 1992; Doyle, *Kant, Liberal Legacies and Foreign Affairs*.
6　Huntington, *Clash of Civilisations*, p. 12.
7　Mearsheimer, *Back to the Future*, p. 12.
8　*Ibid*.
9　Waltz, *The Emerging Structure*.
10　T. Smith, 'In Defense of Interventionism', *Foreign Affairs*, 1994, 73(6), pp. 34–47, at p. 35.
11　J.R. Huntley, *Pax Democratica: A Strategy for the 21st Century*, Basingstoke, Macmillan, 1998, p. 164.
12　K. Roth, 'Sidelined on Human Rights: America Bows Out', *Foreign Affairs*, 1998, 77(2), pp. 2–6, at p. 2.
13　B. Buzan, *People, States and Fear*, Hemel Hempstead, Simon and Schuster, 1991.
14　D. Baldwin, 'The Concept of Security', *Review of International Studies*, 1997, 23, pp. 5–26; L. Friedman, 'International Security: Changing Targets', *Foreign Policy*, 1998, 110, pp. 48–63.
15　C. Weinberger, *Fighting for Peace: Seven Critical Years in the Pentagon*, New York, Warner Books, 1990.
16　C. Powell, 'Enormous Power, Sobering Responsibility', *Foreign Affairs*, 1992, 70(5), pp. 32–46, at p. 38.
17　*Ibid*., p. 39.
18　C. Powell, *A Soldier's Way*, London, Hutchinson, 1995, p. 424.
19　*Ibid*., p. 425.
20　Warren Christopher, 'America's Leadership: America's Opportunity', *Foreign Policy*, 1995, 98, p. 8.
21　Quoted from C.W. Kegley and E.R. Wittkopf, *World Politics: Trend and Transformation*, New York, St. Martin's, 5th edition 1995, p. 415.
22　W. Bass, 'The Triage of Dayton', *Foreign Affairs*, 1998, 77(5), pp. 95–108, at p. 99.

Further reading

In a work like this, which can only be footnoted sparingly, it is not possible to acknowledge all we owe to previous scholarship, but we would like to put on record our deep sense of indebtedness. We also offer a select bibliography, in addition to the literature cited throughout the text, as a general guide to further reading.

For an excellent reference book, we recommend B.W. Jentleson & T.G. Paterson (eds.), *Encyclopaedia of U.S. Foreign Relations*, 4 vols., New York, US Council of Foreign Relations, Oxford University Press, 1997. For ready access to primary sources, see the *Foreign Relations of the United States*, which contains a wealth of published US diplomatic documents, at <http://www.state.gov/www/about state/history/index.html> and then go to FRUS in the index; and the Cold War International History Project at < cwihp.si.edu >.

Broad overviews of post-war US foreign policy include Walter Lafeber, *The American Age: United States Foreign Policy at Home and Abroad Since 1750*, New York, Norton & Norton, 1989; G. Kolko, *Confronting the Third World: United States Foreign Policy, 1945–1980*, New York, Pantheon Books, 1988; T. J. McCormick, *America's Half-Century: United States Foreign Policy in the Cold War*, Baltimore, Hopkins University Press, 1989; S.E. Ambrose, *Rise to Globalism*, Harmondsworth Middlesex, Penguin, 1988; James E. Dougherty and Robert L. Pfaltzgraff, *American Foreign Policy: FDR to Reagan*, New York, Harper Row, 1986; J. Dumbrell, *American Foreign Policy: Carter to Clinton*, London, Macmillan, 1997.

For the traditions, formulation, and control of American foreign policy see F.H. Hartmann & R.L. Wendzel, *America's Foreign Policy in a Changing World*, New York, Harper Collins, 1994; C.W. Kegley Jr. & E.R. Wittkopf, *American Foreign Policy: Pattern and Process*, 7th edit., London, Macmillan, 1999; J.T. Rourke, *Presidential Wars and American Democracy: Rally 'Round the Chief*, New York, Paragon House, 1992;

M. Nincic, *Democracy and Foreign Policy: the Fallacy of Political Realism*, New York, Columbia University Press, 1992; J.A. Rosati, *The Politics of United States Foreign Policy*, New York, Harcourt Brace Jovanovich, 1993; & J.A. Rosati (ed.), *Readings in the Politics of the United States*, New York, Harcourt Brace Jovanovich, 1998.

For the international system see H. Bull, *The Anarchical Society: A Study of Order in World Politics*, London, Macmillan, 1977; C.W. Kegley & C. Wittkopf, *World Politics: Trend and Transformation*, 7th edit., London, Macmillan, 1999; D. Baldwin (ed.), *Neorealism and Neoliberalism: The Contemporary Debate*, New York, Columbia University Press, 1992; K. Booth & S. Smith (eds.), *International Relations Theory Today*, Cambridge, Polity Press, 1995; Paul R. Viotti & Mark V. Kauppi, *International Relations Theory: Realism, Pluralism, Globalism, and Beyond*, Boston, Allyn & Bacon, 1999.

For the general Cold War era, students should be aware that academic work is vast and divided by an ongoing interpretative debate between: traditionalists, revisionists, post-revisionists, corporatists, and world systems theorists. For an introduction to the origins of the Cold War see M.P. Lefler & D.S. Painter (eds.), *Origins of the Cold War: An International History*, London, Routledge, 1994. The seminal text on containment policy remains J.L. Gaddis, *Strategies of Containment. A Critical Appraisal of Postwar American National Security Policy*, Oxford, Oxford University Press, 1982. For very different interpretations of the origins of US Cold War foreign policy see H. Feis, *From Trust to Terror, 1945–50*, NewYork, W.W. Norton, 1970; W. Appleman Williams, *The Tragedy of American Diplomacy*, 2nd edit., New York, Dell Publishing, 1972; D. Yergin, *Shattered Peace: The Origins of the Cold War and the National Security State*, Boston, Houghton Mifflin, 1977. For *détente* and the end of the Cold War see Raymond Garthoff, *Détente and Confrontation: American–Soviet Relations from Nixon to Reagan*, Washington DC, Brookings Institute, 1994; M.R. Beschloss & S. Talbott, *At the Highest Levels: The Inside Story of the End of the Cold War*, Boston, Little, Brown, 1993; Michael J. Hogan (ed.), *The End of the Cold War: Its Meaning and Implications*, New York, CUP, 1992; Richard Ned Lebow & Janice Gross Stein, *We All Lost the Cold War*, Princeton, Princeton UP, 1994. Finally, for two interesting retrospectives see J.L. Gaddis, *We Now Know: Rethinking Cold War History*, Oxford, Clarendon Press, 1997; & A.P Dobson (ed.), with G. Evans and S. Malik (assistant eds.), *Deconstructing and Reconstructing the Cold War*, Aldershot, Ashgate, 1999.

For US economic policy during the Cold War see G. Adler-Karlsson, *Western Economic Warfare, 1947–67: A Case Study in Foreign*

Chile 36, 51, 54, 68–9, 74
China 7, 10, 13, 20, 25, 27, 29, 34–5, 70, 76–9, 81, 85, 87, 89–90, 104, 110, 112–13, 122; conflict with Soviet Union 35; Cultural Revolution 86; Tiananmen Square 90, 113
Christopher, Warren 11, 17, 112, 134
Church, Frank 10
Churchill, Winston 12, 20–1
'clash of civilisations' 118, 127, 137
Clayton, William 22
Clinton, Bill 1, 9, 10, 11, 12, 17, 52, 54, 74, 105–24, 129, 134–5
Coard, Bernard 68
Cold War 10, 12, 16, 18–45, 56–104, 106, 108, 110, 115–16, 118, 122–4, 127–8, 131, 135; Africa, 91–4; Asia 66–90; containment 22–45, 56–103; Europe 18–23, 56–64; Middle East 94–103; NSC (68) 23–6, 29, 33–4, 36, 38–9, 44, 76, 79–81, 88, 94; post-Cold War 7, 16, 104–37; assertive multilateralism 116, 124–5, 129–31, 134; interventionism (US) 124–37; Presidential Directive (25) 122, 130, 135; Second Cold War 30, 37–40, 43, 52; security 131–7; Western Hemisphere 65–75
Commerce Department 11
Conference on Security and Co-operation in Europe 13
Congress 2, 7–10, 16, 24, 33, 36–7, 43, 54–5, 69, 79–80, 84–5, 88–9, 114, 119, 121, 135; bipartisanship 14
Conventional Force Levels in Europe Treaty 42, 109
Coordinating Committee (COCOM) 62, 87
Cordier, Andrew 73
counter-insurgency warfare 32, 83; see also Vietnam War
Cruise missiles 40, 62
Cuba 4, 54, 67–74, 92–3, 105–6, 121; Bay of Pigs 69–70, 83; Cuban missile crisis 2, 7, 12, 31, 40, 60, 70–4
Cyprus 58
Czechoslavakia 57

de Gaulle, Charles 60–2, 82

détente 28, 33–7, 73, 89, 99–100
Diem, Ngo Dinh 83
Dobrynin, Anatoly 73
Dominican Republic 68, 74
domino theory 26, 38, 82
Doyle, Michael 127, 129, 134
Dulles, Allen 66
Dulles, John Foster 10, 11, 26–7, 32, 39, 66, 89, 92

Eagleburger, Lawrence 12, 119, 129
Earth Summit, Rio de Janeiro 121
Egypt 95–8, 100
Eisenhower, Dwight 11, 31, 33, 39, 41, 59, 78, 81–3, 93, 95, 98; Doctrine 14, 97; domino theory 26; New Look 26–9
El Salvador 39, 44, 120
Ethiopia 39, 92–4
Europe 3–4, 27, 105–110; Common Agricultural Policy 49, 60, 63–4, 125; Common Foreign and Security Policy 105–6; Eastern Europe 20, 22–3, 28, 41–2, 44, 50, 105; Economic and Monetary Union 105; European Coal and Steel Community 59–60; European Community 53, 104–5; European Defence Community 58–9, 82, 89; European Economic Community 49–50, 60–1; European Monetary System 52; European Payments Union 59; European Security and Defence Identity 105–6; European Union 1, 54, 105, 122, 137; integration 48, 56, 58–64, 105; Western Europe 20, 22, 34, 39, 43, 65, 85, 89, 101; Western European Union 59, 106; see also European Recovery Program; Marshall Plan
Executive, see Presidency
Executive Committee of the National Security Council (EXCOM) 72–3

Falklands War 74
First World War 4, 122
Ford, Gerald 8, 11, 33–4, 36, 51, 85, 93–4, 99
foreign policy-making 1–17; democratic controls 7–17, 43, 84, 88, 124–37

Index

Acheson, Dean 10, 44, 78–9
Afghanistan 37, 39, 43, 100, 118
Africa 91–4, 103–4, 114–115
Albright, Madeleine 1, 11, 17, 117
Allende, Salvador 36, 69
Andean Pact 119
Anglo–American Special Relationship 58, 62
Anglo–Iranian Oil Company 95, 97
Angola 39
Anti-ballistic missile systems 35
ANZUS Pact 27, 88
Apartheid 91, 104
Arab–Israeli conflicts 1948, 95; 1956, 98; see also, Six Day War; and Yom Kippur War
Arafat, Yasser 101, 116–17
Argentina 74
Armas, Castillo 66
Asia 56, 76–90, 104, 106, 110–114
Asia Pacific Economic Co-operation Forum 53–4, 111
Asian Tigers 51, 104
Association of South East Asian Nations 111, 114
Attlee, Clement 81
Austria 57

Baghdad Pact 27, 97
Baker, James 12, 41
Baldwin, David 131
Barac, Ehud 117
Barshefskay, Charlene 53–4
Batista, Fulgencio 67
Berger, Samuel 11
Berlin, Blockade 12, 22, 56–7;

crisis (1960–62), 31, 57, 60, 70, 83; Wall 64
Bevin, Ernest 95
Bishop, Michael 68
Black Africa 91–2, 102–3, 114
Blair, Tony 107
Bosnia 104, 106, 110, 121, 134–6; Dayton Accords 106–7, 134; US intervention 134–5; Vance–Owen Peace Plan 107
Brandt, Willy 61
Bretton Woods System 48–50, 58, 61
Brezhnev, Leonid 35; Doctrine 42
Brown, Harold 87
Brussels Treaty 59
Brzezinski, Zbigniew 11–12
Bundy, McGeorge 11
Bush, George 12, 40–4, 105, 107–9, 111–24, 132–4
Buzan, Barry 131

Cabral, Donald Reid 68
Cambodia 14, 82, 84, 87
Canada 52–3
Carter, Jimmy 3, 11, 33–4, 36–8, 51, 62, 74, 85, 87, 93–4, 100, 102, 120; Doctrine, 14, 100–1
Case–Zablocki Act 8, 15
Castro, Fidel 10, 67–9, 72, 74, 105, 121
Central Intelligence Agency 10, 13, 28, 36, 39, 66–70, 83, 97, 100
Central Treaty Organisation 27, 33, 97
Chechen War 109–10
Cheney, Richard 42, 111
Chiang, Kai-shek 25, 77–8, 80, 88

The United States and Japan Since the Occupation, New York, Oxford University Press, 1997; W.I. Cohen, *The United States and Japan in the Post War World*, Lexington Ky, University Press of Kentucky, 1989; G. Chang, *Friends and Enemies: The United States, China, and the Soviet Union, 1948–1972*, Stanford, Stanford University Press, 1990; G.A. James, *The China Connection: US Policy and the Peoples Republic of China*, Stanford, Stanford University Press, 1986; A.X. Jiang, *The United States and China*, Chicago, Chicago University Press, 1988; J.G. Stoessinger, *Nations at Dawn: China, the United States, and the Soviet Union,* 6th edit., New York, McGraw Hill, 1994.

For US relations with Africa see M. Kalb, *Congo Cables: The Cold War in Africa from Eisenhower to Kennedy*, New York, Macmillan, 1982; T.J. Noer, *Cold War and Black Liberation: The United States and White Rule in Africa, 1948–68*, Columbia, Mo., University of Missouri Press, 1985; R.C. Coker, *The United States and South Africa 1968–85: Constructive Engagement and its Critics*, Durham North Carolina, Duke Press, 1986; R.K. Massie, *Loosing the Bonds: The United States and South Africa During the Apartheid Years*, New York, 1997; T. Borstelmann, *Apartheid's Reluctant Uncle: The United States and Southern Africa in the Early Cold War*, Oxford, Oxford University Press, 1993; P.J. Schraeder, *United States Foreign Policy toward Africa: Incrementalism, Crisis and Change*, Cambridge, Cambridge University Press, 1994.

For the US and the Middle East see W. Stivers, *America's Confrontation with Revolutionary Change in the Middle East, 1948–83,* London, Macmillan, 1986; R. Ovendale, *Origins of the Arab Israeli Wars*, London, Longman, 1984; B.I. Kaufman, *The Arab Middle East and the United States: Inter-Arab Rivalry and Super-Power Diplomacy*, New York, Twayne, 1996; S.L. Spiegel, *The Other Arab–Israeli Conflict: Making America's Middle East Policy from Truman to Reagan*, Chicago, University of Chicago Press, 1985; H.W. Brands, *Into the Labyrinth: The United States and the Middle East, 1945–1993*, New York, McGraw Hill, 1994; L.T. Hardar, *Quagmire: America in the Middle East*, Washington, D.C., Cato Institute, 1992; R.O. Freedman (ed.), *The Middle East from the Iran–Contra Affair to the Intifada*, New York, Syracuse University Press, 1991.

For the American experience in the Western Hemisphere see G.T. Allison, *Essence of Decision: Explaining the Cuban Missile Crisis*, Boston, Little, Brown, 1971; C. J. Arnson, *Crossroads: Congress, the Reagan Administration, and Central America*, New York, Pantheon Books, 1989; R.L. Garthoff, *Reflections on the Cuban Missile Crisis*, Washington, D.C., Brookings Institute, 1989; J.J. Johnson, *A Hemisphere*

Economic Policy, Stockholm, Almquist &Wiksell, 1968; Diane Kunz, *Butter and Guns: America's Cold War Economic Diplomacy,* New York, Free Press, 1997; A.P. Dobson, *The Politics of the Anglo-American Economic Special Relationship*, Brighton, Wheatsheaf, 1988, and his *US Economic Statecraft 1933–1990: Policies of Economic Warfare and Strategic Embargo,* London, Routledge, forthcoming; P.J. Fungiello, *American–Soviet Trade During the Cold War,* Chapel Hill, University of North Carolina Press, 1988; M. Mastanduno, *Economic Containment: COCOM and the Politics of East–West Trade*, Ithaca, Cornell University Press, 1992; J.E. Spero & Jeffrey A. Hart, *The Politics of International Economic Relations*, 5th edit., London, Routledge, 1997.

For US relations with Western Europe see G. Lundestad, *"Empire" by Integration: The United States and European Integration, 1945–1997*, Oxford, Oxford University Press, 1998; & his (ed.), *No End to Alliance. The United States and Western Europe: Past, Present and Future*, London, Macmillan, 1998; J. Joffe, *The Limited Partnership. Europe, the United States, and the Burdens of Alliance*, Cambridge, Mass., Ballinger, 1987; M. Hogan, *The Marshall Plan: America, Britain, and the Reconstruction of Western Europe, 1947–52*, Cambridge, Cambridge University Press, 1987; Alan Milward, *The Reconstruction of Western Europe 1945–51*, London, Methuen, 1984; C.S. Maier (ed.), *The Cold War in Europe: Era of a Divided Continent*, Princeton, Weiner, 1996; P. Winand, *Eisenhower, Kennedy, and the United States of Europe*, London, Macmillan, 1997; R.L. Rubenstein (ed.), *The Dissolving Alliance: The United States and the Future of Europe*, New York, Paragon House, 1987; W. Goldstein (ed.), *Reagan's Leadership and the Atlantic Alliance: Views From Europe and America*, London, Pergammon-Brassey, 1986; S. Gill (ed.), *Atlantic Relations: Beyond the Reagan Era*, New York, St. Martin's, 1989; K. Featherstone & R. Ginsberg, *The United States and the European Union in the 1990s: Partners in Transition*, London, Macmillan, 1996.

For Asia, good starting points are M. Hastings, *The Korean War*, London, Michael Joseph, 1987; R.J. Foot, *The Wrong War: American Policy and Dimensions of the Korean Conflict*, Ithaca, N.Y., Cornell University Press, 1985; B. Cumings, *The Origins of the Korean War, Vol. 2, The Roaring of the Cataract*, Princeton, Princeton University Press, 1992; G.C. Herring, *America's Longest War: The United States and Vietnam 1950–1975*, New York, Wiley, 1979; G. Lewy, *America in Vietnam: Illusion, Myth, and Reality*, New York, Oxford University Press, 1978; G. Kahin, *Intervention: How America became Involved in Vietnam*, New York, Knopf, 1986; W. LaFeber, *The Clash: A History of US–Japanese Relations*, New York, W.W. Norton, 1997; M. Schaller, *Altered States:*

tends to be a simplicity of faith in the criteria for intervention and exit strategies.

As we wrote the closing pages of the penultimate draft of this book, Richard Holbrooke had just failed, after valiant efforts, to persuade Presidents Milosevic to stop the Yugoslav Serb army from attacking the Albanian minority in Kosovo. NATO, under US command, was conducting aerial attacks against the Serbs in Kosovo. No-one knew what the outcome might be. No-one knew whether or not ground troops would have to go in. Once in, no-one knew how NATO would get them out. If the situation proved intractable and there were a long drawn out military struggle, some would have said that NATO left intervention until it was too late, others that NATO should never have gone in. Some would have said air strikes were inadequate as a strategy and that ground troops should have gone in from the start, others would have protested about the danger of provoking the Russians. We now know that after a longer period of air strikes than many had expected, with a growing threat that ground troops would go in and pressures from Russia, Milosevic eventually gave way. Nevertheless, these are the problems of interventionism in the starkest and most basic form.

There are no clear and simple answers to the problems of interventionism. All interventions have as their goal the restitution or creation of a new kind of order. But there are two fundamental problems with this. Cultural differences produce both problems for the understanding and the management of the situation and disputes about what nature that order should take. Second, intervention, by definition, is something short of conquest: at some point those who intervene must withdraw. At the end of the day, after the exit strategy has been successfully executed, the future of whatever has been achieved has to be placed in the hands of some indigenous party. The future is beyond control, unless a state is prepared to intervene again. Attention might thus be most appropriately directed, not at efficient exit strategies, but at what happens afterwards. This is not to say that interventions should never be mounted. Rather, it is to say that, as the Panamanian, Bosnian and Kosovan experiences demonstrate, they are always more complex, fraught with unexpected dangers, and complicated by dilemmas of moral choice than any formula or model can capture. Such complexity and dangers suggest that more reserve is required than has been in evidence in much recent literature, which sees the present world situation as an opportunity for the US to take an aggressive lead in defending and spreading the benefits of liberal democracy abroad.

way to Bosnia whether the administration liked it or not. The confusion stemmed from an earlier presidential decision that, should the situation on the ground become chaotic ..., NATO would intervene to help the blue helmets flee. ... While an intervention to limit U.N. failure would be dangerous and humiliating, the White House figured that reneging on its promise to NATO would destroy the remains of its credibility and devastate an already frayed alliance. ... What one Clinton adviser called "the single most difficult decision of [Clinton's] presidency – to send troops to Bosnia" has been made without anyone realizing it.[22]

Neither ideology nor realist self-interest seem able to explain this. Instead, US intervention was the result of contingency and a lack of careful consideration of what appeared to be a limited engagement (to help UN forces pull out). Clinton had declared that there were no directly threatened US interests. Democratic enlargement was hardly a primary consideration and humanitarian concerns emerged only rather belatedly. Nothing more than lip-service was paid to either exit strategy, or to the cautionary language of Presidential Directive 25, issued in the wake of Somalia. Finally, both public opinion and the Congress were initially opposed to US troop involvement and capability was never an issue.

Where does all this leave US policy and its criteria for intervention in regional crises? The conflicting models of what the world out there is really like, and the debate about what the new security agenda should be, may have puzzled US policy-makers more than it has helped them. This is particularly worrying when the question of US capabilities seems to have been decided, for the present, in favour of US ability to act widely in the international sphere either unilaterally or multilaterally. In other words, with US intervention capability intact and with inhibitions about intervention weakening as Vietnam recedes, as traditional notions of sovereignty wane, and as the end of the Cold War has removed the possibility of countermoves by another superpower, the time for US interventionism appears to be ripe. Furthermore, the current US style and rhetoric reinforce this. Wilsonian idealism has revived and gained leverage, partly because it seems a more realistic programme than before to try to implement US democratic and free market ideals globally. In weighing up whether or not to take action, the scales seem to be on a table tilted in favour of intervention. However, while many idealists feel that it should be tilted in this way, it is instructive to note that its intellectual foundations are shaky, the prevailing rhetoric can confuse, complicate and mislead, and hopes for multilateralism seem over-optimistic and based on an over-simplistic analysis. Even when decisions about intervention are made on less emotive or pragmatic grounds, there still that other largely symbolic features of decline, such as the burning with impunity of the Stars and Stripes in Teheran in 1980, had been grossly exaggerated. The US did have a substantial problem in the form of debts bequeathed to the nation by the Reagan administration, but there was a remedy. Resources should be shifted from consumption to investment in industry and education. That would enable Americans to afford both social and international security. Above all, they should not cut themselves off from the international environment because it is a vital factor for both US strength and security. In short, the US must not lose faith because it is still 'bound to lead'.

By the end of the millennium, it looked as if Kennedy had got things drastically wrong and Nye more or less right. The Soviet Union imploded in 1991 and Russia has been in disarray ever since. In 1989, the US economy, with a GDP of $5.2 trillion, was still 1.8 times the size of Japan's, its nearest rival. By 1995, it had grown 30% to $7 trillion. In contrast, the Japanese economy grew 4% and Germany's 5%. The US trade deficit was $100 billion in 1995 (and set to rise to $300 billion in 1999), but that was partly offset by a $80 billion surplus on services, banking and royalties. Furthermore, US factories abroad command a greater share of world exports than their domestic counterparts, which means that the US overall, on these calculations, makes a modest profit on its dealings with the global economy. When these traditional indicators of economic power are added to the new forms of power identified by Susan Strange – production, financial, and knowledge structures – then, one begins to realise the overstated nature of Kennedy's thesis. And there is more. In 1998 Congress appropriated $247 billion for defence. That was only 15% of the federal budget, but about equivalent to the defence expenditure of the next ten biggest military powers added together. On top of all this, the US has a flexible economy, a political, social and cultural environment that continues to attract many of the world's best and brightest, and positions of established influence and power in all the world's great organisations. The US is not going to be any less important in world affairs for the foreseeable future or less powerful in the deliberations of the international system. Without doubt, it has the wherewithal to intervene with great power anywhere in the world. So, rumours of decline seem to have been grossly exaggerated, but it should also be noted that US strength is now intertwined inextricably with the fortunes of the world outside its boundaries: the neo-isolationist option is not real. But what is the world out there like on which the US now depends and in which it might have cause to intervene forcibly from time to time? What kind of security, or other, considerations might legitimately impel it to do so?

consider matters at a more thematic level to try to capture significant post-Cold War changes that have affected US foreign policy and identify the most important challenges for the future. In doing so we shall examine: US capabilities; the nature of the post-Cold War world and the new security agenda; and the general character of the US response to the new dispensation, with specific reference to military intervention in other states. This last focus of attention has been chosen because, in many ways, it encapsulates the most complex of foreign policy challenges and highlights the problem of exercising democratic control over those who make such decisions. How a state intervenes forcibly in the affairs of another and the justification it offers say much about the character of its foreign policy and of the values and character of the state itself.

Capability

As the Cold War faded away Paul Kennedy wrote *The Rise and Fall of the Great Powers*, which elaborated a theory of inevitable imperial overstretch. This intensified arguments about US relative decline and fed into a wider debate about hegemony.

In 1945, the US had 40% of the world's wealth and was painlessly able to devote 9–10% of GNP to defence during the 1950s and 1960s. This declined to 6–7% by the 1980s, but its overall wealth slumped more dramatically from 40% to 20–24% of the world total. As a result, Kennedy announced: 'decision makers in Washington must now face the awkward and enduring fact that the sum total of the United States' global interests and obligations is nowadays far larger than the country's power to defend them all simultaneously.'[3]

Economic omens were certainly not good. High technology trade slipped from a US surplus of $27 to $4 billion between 1980 and 1985. US strength in agricultural exports was undermined by the EC CAP and by rising Third World productivity. Turbulence in national finances caused high interest rates and an overvalued dollar, which diminished export markets. And finally, the US plunged further into debt. By 1985 the annual trade deficit was over $200 billion and the national debt stood at $1.8 trillion, which carried interest charges of $129 billion a year. The US, it seemed, was fated to go the way of all empires: it would decline.

Responses to Kennedy came most notably from Joseph S. Nye.[4] He pointed out that if Kennedy had taken a pre-war baseline for calculating US wealth, then its relative decline would have been insignificant. It was only because the economies of other industrial nations had not recovered from the devastation of the Second World War, that the relative power of the US was so unnaturally inflated in the late 1940s. Nye also claimed case of Clinton, dither indecisively, sometimes with grave consequences. For example, in 1994 Clinton put forward both Presidential Directive 25, which restricted US participation in collective security, and a National Security document entitled 'A Strategy for Engagement and Enlargement'.

Is it fair, though, to castigate either US policy-makers for inconsistencies and their failure to deliver a New World Order, or Clinton personally for reneging on idealistic commitments, such as linking human rights to China's MFN status? As far as the American people are concerned, almost certainly not. They have been concerned about domestic issues and unwilling to sanction a global policeman role for the US at a time when it heads for a $300 billion trade deficit. Bush and Clinton have therefore had to balance carefully US interests against both constrained resources and a lack of popular support for military interventions. As for Clinton's conversion from idealist to foreign affairs pragmatist, this has done him no harm whatsoever. A recent survey revealed that he had made a dramatic comeback from being ranked eighth of very successful US Presidents on foreign policy in 1994 to first at the end of 1998.[16] Furthermore, much of what has been witnessed in the 1990s has been beyond American control. The US cannot be held responsible for Milosevic's ethnic cleansing in Kosovo, the lack of popular support for the Middle Eastern peace process, Iraqi defiance of the UN, instability in Russia, or the refusal of states such as India and Pakistan to abide by the Nuclear Non Proliferation Treaty. The need has therefore been to fashion a response to a world which still often rejects American values and in which even US allies pose major challenges.

Bush and Clinton have certainly got many things wrong. The current relationship with Russia is a long retreat from strategic partnership, US–Japanese trade relations have become mutually antagonistic, and the bilateral relationship with the EU 'is drifting dangerously toward crisis.'[17] Likewise, as Chapter 10 demonstrates in detail, the US has yet to come to terms with the new issues, the strategic uncertainty, and its own role in the new multipolar structure. However, judgement on post-Cold War American foreign policy must be made by the individual and in the context of what is, rather than what ought to be. In many ways the aftermath of the Cold War has reflected those of the First and Second World Wars. After each, there were hopes for a new and better world order, and each time these crumbled amid state rivalries and a recognition that there is no common vision of an acceptable world order. As America, the last superpower, enters the new millennium, it is destined to labour under the combined weight of global expectation and increasing challenge to its position. The immediate threats it faces may be less, but the challenges of advantage left Bush embarrassingly isolated in resisting measures on global warming and biodiversity. Third, the US has found difficulty in responding effectively to some items on the new security agenda. The 'drug war' launched by President Bush in 1990 is a clear example. Despite spending more than $70 billion on fighting drugs and attaching conditionality clauses on aid to countries such as Peru and Bolivia, the US has had little effect other than to lower the street price of drugs and stimulate coca and poppy production. Finally, the problems of blurring domestic and foreign policy have been particularly pronounced in US policies in the Western Hemisphere. Clinton's early ideas to develop more communication with the Cuban civilian population were scrapped in the face of a strong anti-Castro movement in Congress. Instead, Clinton, following Cuba's shooting down of two small planes violating its air space, signed the Helms–Burton bill in March 1996 which tightened the embargo and precluded any negotiations until Castro fell from power. Consequently, domestic political consider-ations have left Cuba conspicuously omitted from US efforts to engage communist and former communist countries, and have placed the US both in breach of international law and at loggerheads with allies who want to trade with Cuba.

Conclusion

Anyone looking for a US-led New World Order will be bitterly disap-pointed by American foreign policy in the 1990s. Bush and Clinton both talked of this and at times leaned toward the assertive multilateralism required to push it forward: the 1990 Gulf War, Somalia, belated inter-vention in Bosnia, and more convincingly in Kosovo. However, palpable failings illustrate the lack of will to follow through when US national interests are not directly threatened. This is epitomised by congressional aid cuts to the Third World, by presidential passivity in the face of mass genocide in Rwanda, and by a lack of US leadership in addressing con-troversial items on the new security agenda – such as at the 1992 Earth Summit, where George Bush refused to make any commitments regard-ing biodiversity and climate change. Anyone who expected consistency in post-Cold War US foreign policy would likewise be disappointed. The direction, however faulty, provided by containment and a bipolar power configuration has been replaced by an inchoate blend of contradictory American values, the blurring of domestic and foreign policy, and mounting challenges, especially economic, to US predominance. The product has been an *ad hoc* approach to foreign policy that has seen US administrations embrace contradictory policies and, particularly in the

interests. China has formally agreed to move toward a strategic partnership with Russia in the next century, continues to posture over Taiwan,
and has embraced an authoritarian developmental model ill-suited to US
international trade liberalisation. The US has responded by reaffirming
its commitment to Taiwan, trying to consolidate its relationship with
Japan and other ASEAN members, and vigorously defending its economic interest *vis-à-vis* China – such as intellectual property rights.
However, while the US is not prepared to pursue engagement at any
price, it has been prepared to do so at the expense of human rights and
American principles. In 1994 Clinton renewed China's MFN status and,
against the tide of American public opinion, de-coupled the issues of
trade and human rights. Two years later, his conversion from idealist to
pragmatist was confirmed when the US refused to apply sanctions on
China for its export of M-11 missiles and strategically important ring
magnets to Pakistan.

Middle East and Africa

American attitudes to Africa and the Middle East remain very different.
Africa has benefited little from either the blurring of foreign and domestic policy or the shift from geopolitics to geoeconomics. Bush set the
tone of America's African policy: it was confused and erratic. There
were elements of idealism: support for the reversal of apartheid in South
Africa and warnings that anti-communist dictatorial regimes would no
longer qualify automatically for US aid. At the same time, the foundation of problems for future US interventionism were unwittingly laid
when Bush mounted Operation Restore Hope in December 1992, which
sent 28,000 American troops, operating under a UN resolution, to aid
food distribution in Somalia. Finally, there emerged a hierarchy of interests. For example, in 1992 South Africa appeared on the US Commerce
Department's list of twelve Big Emerging Markets whilst Black Africa
was put 'onto America's "back burner"'.[13]

Clinton has accelerated these trends. The US has continued to support
sustainable development and democratisation by attaching stricter con-
ditionality clauses to aid and through indirect means, such as encouragement of UN initiatives in Rwanda, assistance to Italian mediators in
Mozambique, and support for Nigerian efforts to broker the Sudan conflict. Clinton has also continued the trend toward a differentiated African
policy and its marginalisation within US considerations, a move assisted
when Congress was seized in November 1994 by Republicans who were
reluctant to commit US money to overseas development projects. In
1995, Clinton allocated just 12% of a shrinking foreign aid budget to

between regional stability and conflict. China's marriage of market economy with authoritarian leadership has produced an average growth rate of 8-10% between 1978 and 1997. It has also attracted in excess of $100 billion of direct foreign investment, created a trade surplus with the US second only to Japan's, and secured the reversion of prestigious Hong Kong from British control. China's rise has put it at the heart of Asian security too. Sino-American co-operation could significantly ease difficulties, such as with the US–North Korean agreement of 1994 to stop the latter's military nuclear programme. As a permanent member of the UN Security Council, a nuclear power, and a leading international arms supplier, China's co-operation is also of great importance in arms control, nuclear non-proliferation, and the promotion of multilateral co-operation in Asia. The obverse of this is China's potential to create major regional instability. Its posture of non-aggressiveness is often difficult to reconcile with its claims to large parts of the South China Sea, its 40% increase in military expenditure between 1990 and 1995, and its provocative acts, such as testing missiles in July 1995 near Taiwan. It also continues its development of nuclear capabilities – a particularly sensitive issue in light of revelations in April 1999 of Chinese espionage in America's nuclear programme. There are also fears that China might adopt similar policies toward Taiwan to those used to reclaim Hong Kong and the Portuguese territory of Macau, which reverted to China on 20 December 1999.

The US response to the 'China challenge' has again been marked by Bush pragmatism and Clinton's betrayal of electoral promises. The honeymoon period in Sino-American relations coincided with Deng Xiaoping's programme of economic reform and international engagement during the 1980s and was largely over even before the Cold War ended. American calculations of the strategic triangle were replaced by concern for regional stability and an anxiety to expand trade links. Bush therefore advocated 'constructive engagement' with China and made a very pragmatic, muted response to the human rights issue epitomised by the Tiananmen Square massacre on 4 June 1989. Clinton attacked Bush for this *realpolitik* approach, promised to pursue with all vigour US principles in his dealings with China, and expressed a desire to link human rights with China's MFN status. Such idealism has proved to be empty rhetoric and Clinton has admitted that 'it would be fair to say that my policies with regard to China have been somewhat different from what I talked about in the [1992 presidential] campaign.'[12] Constructive engagement has continued to dominate Sino-American relations, with Clinton anxious both to accommodate and contain China. There is no automatic Sino-American coincidence of either economic or security

9   The US and the post-Cold War disorder

The startling implosion of the Soviet Union and the end of the Cold War revolutionised the context in which US foreign policy had to be developed. Presidents were no longer guaranteed congressional support for intervention overseas and faced public demand for a peace dividend and long overdue redress of domestic problems. Bipolar stability was supplanted by a disorientating and potentially dangerous nascent multipolarity. And containment was suddenly obsolete. This meant both that after 45 years the US had to redefine its foreign policy objectives and that the subsequent prosecution of its interests would be far more difficult. American leaders could no longer use the communist threat to justify almost any action, however blatantly self-interested or immoral, that they cared to take.

The issues and dilemmas of where, when and how to act in a post-Cold War world are examined in detail in Chapter 10, with particular reference to Panama, Bosnia, and Kosovo. But before that, it is necessary to appreciate the enormity of what faced US policy-makers. There was Gorbachev, seemingly intent upon fundamental reform of the Soviet Union but also charged with the uncertain task of redefining its role. As superpower rivalry faded, the US faced both a weakening Cold War alliance structure and a new and more difficult security agenda that included terrorism, drug trafficking, economic globalisation, nuclear proliferation and ecopolitics. And there were new regional problems too. In Europe there was a reunified Germany, a more assertive EC, a destabilising socio-economic divide between East and West, and a geostrategic vacuum in Central and Eastern Europe left by the disintegrating Soviet Union. In Asia there was the rise of China, the challenge of the tiger economies, an increasingly fractious relationship with Japan, and a history of regional instability that was liable to spark new hostilities. In Africa there were questions of what to do about apartheid and the distasteful regimes that the US had supported against communism. In the Middle East there was the rise of Islamic fundamentalism, continuing revealed the conflicting strands of US foreign policy thinking, the impact of political creed within the White House, and the influence of public opinion, especially the connection between 'Black America' and 'Black Africa'.

Finally, the US erroneously superimposed upon both regions a containment strategy designed to combat communism whilst the peoples of Africa and the Middle East were little concerned with the Cold War. Racism rather than 'red peril', and independence rather than colonialism dominated African thinking, and the Arab–Israeli conflict preoccupied Middle Eastern minds. To make matters worse, the US was integrally involved in these problems too – particularly because of its special links with Israel and White South Africa. This crosscutting of issues compromised US policies and caused serious problems within both regions. The Americans and the Soviets played a superpower game using native states as pawns, and the native states fought their own internecine battles and used the superpowers to press their interests. Moreover, even when the Cold War ended, the Americans faced many of the same problems in the Middle East and Africa as they had in 1945. The plight of Black Africa was little improved. Apartheid continued in South Africa. And the only real change in the Middle East was that the US now stood as the region's hegemon and, stripped of its ideological justification for its role there, faced difficult choices as the world entered the post-Cold War era.

guise of Truman's 1949 China White Paper sought in vain to explain this to an enraged American public. Mao's victory had enormous implications for American domestic and foreign policy. Coming as it did in the same year as the Soviet atomic bomb and revelations about espionage in the wartime Manhattan nuclear research project, the loss of China led to an orgy of American recriminations. These were nowhere more vitriolic and influential than in the McCarthy communist witch-hunts, which sought to explain US setbacks as the work of spies and traitors. It was a grandiose conspiracy theory which never stood up to critical analysis, but which appealed, nevertheless, with such force that it wreaked havoc upon both the Truman administration and, ironically, American civil liberties. The State Department was wastefully purged of its China specialists, and government officials, military personnel and defence contractors all had to take loyalty oaths. After these were extended to their families, over twenty million American citizens had been subjected to investigative procedures.[2]

In foreign affairs, McCarthyism helped to tie the hands of American policy-makers. Containment became an intolerant and blinkered strategy which, in the name of democracy and freedom, imprisoned American society for two decades and helped to divide the world with an unforgiving simplicity. It also fathered ill-considered policies. For example, the Americans knew that throughout the Second World War, Stalin had been unsympathetic to Mao and had actually sent aid to the Kuomintang, knowing full well that Chiang would use it against the communists. They knew, too, that after the war the Russians had looted Manchuria and created enormous resentment amongst the Chinese. Furthermore, US allies, notably Britain, told the Truman administration not to regard China and Russia as inevitable partners. Yet, American policy-makers either remained blind to, or were precluded by American public opinion from exploiting, the differences between Stalin and Mao. Instead, General Marshall and Secretary of State Dean Acheson testified before the Senate that they would never recognise the existence of Red China. This led to a bizarre situation in which the US continued to regard Chiang's corrupt and vanquished regime on Taiwan as the Government of China and to deny the PRC a seat in the UN. Moreover, there can be no doubt that when Mao concluded a treaty of mutual assistance with Stalin in February 1950, America's shortsighted and doctrinaire policy had helped to push him closer to the Soviets.

The US further antagonised Mao in 1954, when it locked itself to the Nationalist regime by blocking the PRC's attempts to liberate Taiwan and its tiny offshore islands of Quemoy and Matsu. Eisenhower reaffirmed US commitment to Chiang and in January 1955 he secured the Taiwan Straits Resolution from Congress, which was effectively a blank during the Second World War. Here, US fear of communism overcame sentiment and policy-makers helped reconstruct Japan into their foremost Cold War ally in Asia and, ironically, their fiercest economic rival.

The 'loss' of China

In April 1947, a paper by the US Joint Chiefs of Staff ranked Japan, China and Korea as 13th, 14th and 15th respectively in a hierarchy of strategically significant states. The top seven were all in Europe and it was these that were the focus of American attention. However, while the US struggled with the Soviets in Eastern Europe and over Berlin, the Asian position developed in a way that would plague US policy-makers for most of the 1950s and 1960s.

The first major development came in China. Americans have a long history of interest in China, stemming back through early Christian missions, Hay's Open Door Notes, and the 1844 Treaty of Wangxia that accorded the US trade and extraterritorial rights. However, for much of the early twentieth century China was torn by civil war, particularly after the death of Sun Yat Sen. On one side were the dominant nationalists, known as the Kuomintang (KMT), who were headed by Chiang Kai-shek. On the other were the communists (CCP), led by Mao. The Americans favoured Chiang for reasons of ideology and because he led China's fight against Japan in the 1930s. As the Second World War approached, the US thus looked to Chiang as both an ally in the Far East against Japan and as the man to bring China, its market, and its raw materials, into the capitalist community. Indeed, Roosevelt's post-war vision saw China as one of four world policemen, along with Russia, Britain and the US (later expanded to five with the inclusion of France).

With these things in mind, the Americans spent vast amounts of money propping up Chiang, who repaid them by using his best forces against Mao rather than the Japanese. Mao's forces, though, fought both Chiang and the Japanese. Consequently, they captured the nationalist petard and combined it with communist ideology to make sweeping gains throughout the Chinese countryside. As the war ended, General Marshall was charged with the impossible task of brokering a cease-fire between the KMT and CCP. He failed, not least because the US continued to aid Chiang, and China collapsed into bitter civil war.

When Mao forced the KMT to flee to the offshore island of Taiwan in 1949, the Americans had lost China. For some time there had been a certain inevitability about the communist triumph and, without making an unthinkably large military commitment, there was little the US could have done to salvage Chiang's position on the mainland. A lengthy apologetic in the

The Cuban problem remained: its significance was as much symbolic as anything else. The way that the US conceived of its own position in the Western Hemisphere, and trumpeted it abroad, meant that any loss to communism would necessarily be seen as a major defeat. So, the US could not give up after the Bay of Pigs. Kennedy unleashed CIA Operation Mongoose to try to unseat Castro. Or perhaps one should say de-beard him as one plot involved a poison that removed facial hair! These tactics failed, but angered Castro and provoked fear of another invasion and thus led him deeper into the Soviet embrace.

The Cuban missile crisis

Kennedy was told on 15 October 1962 that the Soviets were building medium (MRBM) and intermediate range ballistic missile (IRBM) sites on Cuba.

The context of the crisis not only demonstrates how intermingled US domestic and Cold War issues had become, it also explains much about how events unfolded. Kennedy had come to power with a flamboyant commitment to get America moving again, retake the initiative in the Cold War, and pay any price and bear any burden for the sake of liberty. The world, however, proved to be more intractable than his optimistic 'can-do' rhetoric suggested. Kennedy suffered a series of setbacks. They started with the Bay of Pigs and continued with a difficult summit meeting with Krushchev in Vienna, the Berlin Crisis and the building of the Wall, difficulties in Laos and a deteriorating situation in Vietnam. In none of these did Kennedy perform well. So, when the missiles were discovered on Cuba, there were a number of background considerations that informed his actions. He was politically vulnerable. His performance had not matched his election rhetoric and October 1962 was the eve of the mid-term congressional elections. Kennedy was also aware that he was the first Democrat president since Truman, and Truman had left office under a hail of criticisms about being weak on communism, failing to end the war in Korea, and for losing China to communism. Kennedy's concerns about these things should not be seen solely as selfish political considerations that pushed him into a hard-line response. The radical right in the US was strong and, in his view, dangerous. Two years later, the Republican opponent of Lyndon Johnson, Barry Goldwater, reputedly suggested 'lobbing one into the men's room at the Kremlin', 'one' being a nuclear bomb. The survival of Democrat leadership was seen as important for the continuation of moderate and rational policies as well as for Kennedy's career. In addition, there were other influential factors. Kennedy was part of that generation which had a horror of appeasement

The stories of Chile in 1970–73 and Nicaragua in 1985–86 also have much in common, but this time covert operations by the CIA and the staff of the NSC provide the common thread. In Chile, the US used money to encourage political opposition and its influence to undermine the economy. The aim was to sabotage the government of the freely elected, pro-marxist, President Allende. These policies went on for three years. Then, in 1973, independently of the CIA, but clearly taking advantage of the instability engineered by it, General Augusto Pinochet mounted a successful military coup that brought a reign of oppression and terror to what had previously been one of the most peaceful and progressive of Latin American countries.

The CIA and members of the NSC made arms sales to Iran both to help to free hostages held by Middle East terrorists and to provide money for Contra rebels fighting the marxist Sandinista Government in Nicaragua: all of which was contrary to the explicit wishes of the US Congress. The mission to keep the Western Hemisphere clean of communism had taken on the appearance of a holy war that went beyond formal policy-making and which broke the bounds of constitutional constraints. Intervention as and when necessary was construed so broadly that it increased out of proportion to the threat and became a corruptive force within the US that was of greater danger than the cancer of communism in the Western Hemisphere it was designed to eradicate.

Cuba and problems in the Western Hemisphere

In April 1959, shortly after taking power in Cuba, Fidel Castro visited the US: it was not a success. Dispute still continues as to whether he was pushed away by the Americans, or voluntarily chose communism. It was probably a mixture of both. By February 1960, already colliding with US interests as he tried to assert Cuban control over the economy, Castro turned to the Soviets for help and signed a trade agreement with them. Soviet Premier Nikita Krushchev then provocatively pronounced that the Monroe Doctrine was dead and welcomed Castroite Cuba as a new liberating force in Latin America. The US retaliated. It renounced the Cuban sugar quota, severed diplomatic relations in early 1961, and instigated an economic embargo. Eisenhower also made plans to remove Castro by force through CIA-trained ex-patriot Cuban dissidents. Thus Kennedy, on entering the White House in 1961, came face to face with one of the most volatile issues of his presidency: Cuba and how to deal with it. Much to his later regret, he took the advice of the CIA and accepted an invasion plan laid by his predecessor. It went ahead at the Bay of Pigs on 17 April 1961 in the expectation that it would prompt a popular uprising. Instead, disaster struck. The invaders never got off the beach and there was no uprising.

neither as strong nor as dominant as it had been in 1945. Second, despite US problems, capitalism was immensely successful, but it had created disparities in development, which both impacted harshly on Third World countries and destabilised the international economy. The third difference was that the wartime planners had a clear vision of what was needed, based largely on the economic theory of John Maynard Keynes. Now there was no clear vision. Keynesian theory seemed inappropriate for contemporary problems. Nixon had begun to confront America's economic shortcomings, but his remedies fell far short of solving them. The harsh fact was that the international economic policy of the US had embarked upon a most turbulent sea of troubles with its navigational equipment still in need of repair.

The fall of Bretton Woods heralded a turbulence that spread beyond monetary problems. The US was confronted by new challenges posed by its relative economic decline. It was entwined in economic interdependence and troubled by the severe recession caused by massive fuel price increases triggered by the Arab–Israeli Yom Kippur War in 1973 and sustained by the Organisation of Petroleum Exporting Countries (OPEC) cartel. It was no longer able to absorb economic costs for political pay-offs, as it had done for the sake of the defence of the West and the development of the EEC, nor was it powerful enough to play a dominant economic managerial role. For many, this spelt the end of US economic hegemony. There was now a process of adjustment to influencing rather than dominating the world economy, which was also paralleled by more caution in the making of US foreign commitments and insistence that allies take more responsibility for their own security. Initially, the economic transition was under the constraints of Cold War imperatives, which largely subordinated economic to strategic priorities. After 1991, economic policy, no less than Eastern Europe, was liberated. However, like some of the ex-Soviet bloc states, US economic policy was plagued by contradictions and unsure of where to go.

Challenges from the Third World

The 1970s not only challenged the US, but the whole ethos of Western capitalism. Assaults upon the entrenched position of the West came from writers at home such as Harry Magdoff,[3] who highlighted American economic imperialism and the fact that US 'aid' to developing countries actually extracted handsome profits (see Chapter 6). From abroad, criticism came from the OPEC cartel and the economically underdeveloped non-aligned 'Group of 77', which started to call for a New International Economic Order (NIEO). They wanted exemption from some of the GATT the Bretton Woods system came into full operation and there was renewed momentum for tariff reductions. The Dillon round of the GATT, 1960–62, reduced the rate on manufactured goods by an average of 10%. However, the re-birth of multilateralism coincided with the emergence of serious economic difficulties in the US. Its long period of vast expenditures overseas on defence, economic assistance and aid (by the mid-1990s the total of all such US post-war aid stood at about $360 billion in 1994 prices), and the rise of efficient competitor economies in West Germany and Japan, all began to tell. Also, the creation of the European Economic Community (EEC) in 1957[2] and, more specifically, its intention to create a Common Agricultural Policy (CAP), which threatened the continuation of vast US agricultural sales in Europe, worried the Americans. Throughout the 1950s the US had a balance of payments deficit, though its trade balance was always in healthy, if steadily declining, surplus. However, by 1960 foreign-held dollars exceeded US gold reserves and this led to a loss of confidence and heavy selling, which developed into a run on the dollar.

These economic developments deeply worried President Kennedy and he sought to restructure relations with Western Europe and to renew the drive for freer trade (see Chapter 5). He had little success with restructuring and even the success of the Kennedy GATT round of 1963–67, which cut tariffs on manufactured goods by 35%, was not enough to avert the looming crisis with Bretton Woods multilateralism. The US continued to over-stretch its commitments beyond its resources in the 1960s. President Johnson's escalation of the Vietnam War and his costly Great Society domestic reforms exacerbated the structural problems already evident at the start of the decade. In 1971 the US ran a trade deficit for the first time in the twentieth century, inflation and unemployment were high and the US could no longer sustain the Bretton Woods system because of pressure on the dollar. Things had changed since 1945 and President Nixon dramatically tried to adjust US policies to the new realities. On 15 August 1971, he announced a new economic policy. He imposed a 10% import surcharge and devalued and disengaged the dollar from gold. Later it was floated on the foreign exchanges to find its market value. The US, by 1973, was clearly no longer in charge of its own economic destiny, and, in fact, Nixon's new economics meant the death of Bretton Woods and danger for multilateralism. The stark realities that US economic problems impressed upon its leaders also had important impact on the way Nixon and Kissinger re-crafted US Cold War strategies (see Chapter 3).

The problems confronting the US in the 1970s were similar to those that had confronted its economic planners during the Second World War, but there were three noticeable differences. First, the US economy was the Senate Select Committee on Intelligence chaired by Senator Frank Church. It unveiled illegal Central Intelligence Agency (CIA) operations, including plans to assassinate Fidel Castro, the leader of Cuba, and led directly to the establishment of a permanent bipartisan Senate Intelligence Oversight Committee (1976) and a House counterpart (1977). Nevertheless, these committees have been rendered somewhat ineffective when confronted by members of the Executive who think that their concept of national security trumps constitutional constraints. Thus, the Senate Committee failed to control the shenanigans of the Iran–Contra affair. However, it does have strong powers, including the right to subpoena witnesses and evidence, and an ability to call the Executive to account *ex post facto*. The ultimate sanction against the President lies with the House of Representatives, which has the power of impeachment. It investigates suspicions of executive high crimes or misdemeanours and can use a special prosecutor to do so. In 1974 this led to the downfall of President Nixon and in 1998–99 to unsuccessful proceedings against Clinton. If there is a case to answer, the President is tried by the Senate.

The distribution of power: the executive branch

Although the executive bureaucracy is there to empower, it also checks and controls the President. The State Department is the formal foreign office of the US. In the nineteenth century, it was small, amateurish and had little to do. Its influence depended upon the stature of the Secretary of State. In the twentieth century, it became more professional with the reforms of the 1924 Rogers Act, but senior diplomatic appointments are still often made on political rather than professional criteria.

The Department's fortunes fluctuated in the post-war period. In the early Cold War, President Truman's inexperience of foreign affairs resulted in his heavy reliance on Secretaries of State George Marshall (1947–49) and Dean Acheson (1949–53). That enhanced the status of the Department, but the fall of China in 1949 and the communist witch-hunt, initiated by Senator Joseph McCarthy, reversed its fortunes and led to a purge of many Asian specialists. Although with Secretary of State John Foster Dulles (1953–59) it seemed that power once again emanated from the Department, and indeed it did, this was more because of Dulles than the Department itself. By the early 1960s a further problem arose: an ever increasing tendency of presidents to use the National Security Council (NSC) and the National Security Adviser (NSA), situated within the Executive Office of the President and established by the National Security Act (1947). During the last forty years been entirely successful, partly because of sophistical distinctions between agreements and 'understandings'.

The Senate has constitutionally and traditionally taken the lead in the Congress in foreign policy. Its Foreign Relations Committee is highly regarded and regularly drawn upon by the Executive for advice. In 1995, Chairman Jesse Helms challenged President Clinton's foreign policy establishment with proposed budget cuts and the abolition of the US Agency for International Development (USAID), the US Information Agency (USIA) and the US Arms Control and Disarmament Agency (USACDA). Clinton blocked the more extreme proposals by vetoing the 1996 Foreign Relations Authorization Bill, but $1.7 billion were cut over a five-year period, and only USAID, of the three agencies targeted by Helms, survived as an independent, though diminished, agency. Many have seen such assertiveness by the Congress as symptomatic of foreign policy becoming a more politically contested sphere and one in which executive power has declined in the post-Cold War world.

iii The control of foreign trade and commerce is given by the constitution to the Congress. This has been delegated extensively to the President since the Reciprocal Trade Agreements Act of 1934, but what the Congress can delegate, it can recall. Over the years Congress has insisted: that allies who received aid should embargo trade with communists (the Mutual Defense Assistance Control or Battle Act 1951); on the inclusion of human rights stipulations in trade agreements (the Jackson–Vanik amendment to the 1974 Trade Act, directed against the Soviet Union); on mandating the US Trade Representative (USTR) to retaliate against states using unfair trade practices (clauses 'Super 301' and 'Special 301' of the 1988 Trade Act); and recently it has refused to grant Clinton 'fast track' authority, something invented in 1974 which means that once a trade agreement has been negotiated it has to be accepted or rejected *in toto* by Congress, rather than being subjected to a series of complicating amendments.

iv The power of congressional oversight: this has always existed but on an *ad hoc* basis. Thus in 1934–35 the famous Nye Committee investigated US entry into the First World War and blamed bankers and arms manufacturers for US involvement. In 1987, Senator John Tower led a commission of investigation into the Iran–Contra affair. Such committees and commissions come and go, but in 1974 growing concerns about covert activities resulted in the establishment of

94–5, 97; China White Paper 78;
Doctrine 14, 21–2, 57, 80
Turkey 21, 58, 88, 97; missiles 71, 73

Ukraine 42
United Fruit Company 66
United Nations 1, 13, 20–1, 78, 80–1,
86, 88, 107, 110, 112, 115, 117, 120,
122, 134–5, 137; Resolution (242)
99, 101; Security Council 20, 72, 80,
86, 88, 113
US Commerce Department 53
US Defense Department 11, 112
US economic performance 46–7, 53, 55,
60, 86, 111–12, 124–6
US Trade Representative 9, 53
US Treasury Department 11, 53
U-Thant 73, 83

Vance, Cyrus 11, 51
Vietnam War 6, 7, 8, 14, 28, 30, 33, 35–
7, 39, 43, 49, 70, 73, 76, 79, 81–5,
88–9, 92, 101,
110, 135; Dien Bien Phu 82; Gulf of
Tonkin Resolution 15, 84; Tet
offensive 84; Vietnam syndrome 38,
76; Viet Minh 81–2

Voluntary Export Restraints 53, 55

Waltz, Kenneth 127–9
War Powers Act 8, 15, 33
Warsaw Pact 42, 57
Washington, George 3
Watergate 15, 36–7, 89
Weinberger, Caspar 38, 101; Doctrine
132
Western Hemisphere 4, 65–75, 105,
118–21, 133; Central America 43;
Latin America 32, 65–75
Wilson, Woodrow 4; Fourteen Points 4
World Trade Organisation 47–8, 54–5,
105

Xiaoping, Deng 113

Yalta Conference 19
Yeltsin, Boris 12, 108–10
Yom Kippur War 35, 50, 62, 99, 101
Yugoslavia 57

Zionisim 91

Organisation of Petroleum Exporting Countries 50–1
Organisation for Security and Co-operation in Europe 106

Pakistan 97, 114, 118, 122
Palestine 95, 101; Liberation Organisation 101, 116–17; Mandate 95
Panama 39, 42, 104–5; Canal 65, 66, 68; Treaties 74, 120; US intervention (Operation Just Cause) 119–20, 132–3, 136
Paris Summit (1960) 28
Paul, Pope John 74
Pearl Harbor 4, 13
Peres, Shimon 117
Pershing II missiles 39–40, 87
Pinochet, Augusto 69
Pleven Plan 59
Poland 18–19, 21
Portugal 56
Portuguese Africa, liberation of 92, 94
Potsdam Conference 21
Powell, Colin 132–3
presidency 8, 10–16; Commander in Chief 7, 8, 14–15; Imperial Presidency 15, 43, 84, 88, 137; Presidential Directive (25) 122, 130, 135
Putin, Vladimir 110

Rabin, Yitzhak 116–17
Reagan, Ronald 11–12, 15, 37–41, 44, 51–2, 62–3, 74, 87, 93–4, 100; Doctrine 14, 37
realism 5–7, 113, 127–9, 137
Reciprocal Trade Agreements Act 9
Reykjavik Summit (1986) 40
Rhee, Singman 79, 81
Ridgway, Matthew 81
Roosevelt, Franklin 12, 19–21, 93
Ross, Dennis 117
Rostow, Walt 32
Rubin, Robert 12, 53
Rusk, Dean 73
Russia 108–110, 114, 122, 136; see also Soviet Union; Chechen War
Rwanda 114–15, 121

Sadat, Anwar 100

Saudi Arabia 98–9
Schultz, George 11, 38
Scowcroft, Brent 133
Second World War 12, 14, 49, 56, 77, 93, 112, 122, 124–5
Senate 2, 8; Foreign Relations Committee 9; Intelligence Oversight Committee 10
Serbia 104, 107, 109
Shcharansky, Anatoly 3
Six Day War 99
Somalia 17, 92–4, 102, 121, 130, 134–5; American deaths in 115; Operation Restore Hope 114
South Africa, Republic of 91, 93, 102, 115
South East Asian Treaty Organisation 27, 33
Soviet Union 3, 13, 18–45, 77, 79, 86–7, 89, 91–6, 98–9, 102–4, 107–8; brigade on Cuba, 74; invasion of Afghanistan 37, 87, 100; SS–20 missiles, 40; see also Russia
Spain 56–7, 88
Stalin, Joseph 12, 19–21, 28, 78, 80
State Department 10, 11, 12, 16, 21, 53, 78, 117, 134; Policy Planning Staff 22–3
Strange, Susan 46
Strategic Arms Limitation Talks 35, 73
Strategic Arms Reduction Talks 40, 42, 108
Strategic Defence Initiative (Star Wars) 37, 39, 87
Stevenson, Adlai 72
Suez Canal 97; Crisis 28, 83, 98, 102
Sung, Kim Il 79–80
Supreme Court 7, 8

Taiwan 25, 27–8, 36, 76–8, 80, 87, 110, 113–14; Quemoy and Matsu 78; Relations Act 89; Resolution 15, 79
Thatcher, Margaret 40, 62
Thieu, Nguyen Van 85
Third World 23, 27, 29, 31–2, 38–9, 41, 50, 58, 67, 76, 83, 89, 121, 125
Tower, John 9
Treaty of Versailles 8
Truman, Harry 10, 11, 19–21, 23, 25–8, 32, 42, 44, 70, 76, 80, 88, 92,

France 19–20, 23, 52, 57–9, 77, 82, 98, 102
Franco–German Treaty of Friendship 60
Free World 24, 44
Freedman, Lawrence 131
Fukuyama, Francis 127, 129, 137

G–7 51, 55
General Agreement on Tariffs and Trade 19, 47–9, 51, 53–4, 61–2, 64; Dillon Round 49, 61; Kennedy Round 49; Tokyo Round 52; Uruguay Round 52, 54
Geneva Summit (1955) 28; Accords 82
Germany 18–22, 41, 58, 104, 108; East Germany 22; reunification 43, 105; West Germany 22, 24–5, 49, 52, 57, 60, 88; West German rearmament 27–8, 58–9, 80
Giap, Vo Nguyen 82
Gill, Stephen 46
Goldwater, Barry 70
Gorbachev, Mikhail 40–3, 107–8, 110; perestroika 42
Great Britain 18–20, 22–3, 52, 57–61, 74, 77–8, 95, 97–8, 102
Greece 21, 57–8, 88, 97
Grenada 39, 44, 68, 74
Group of 77, 50–1
Guatemala 28, 51, 66–7, 74
Guevara, Che 68
Gulf War 8, 42, 116, 121, 124, 133
Guzman, Jacobo Arbentz 66–7

Haig, Alexander 11, 44
Haiti 120
Hay, John 4; Open Door Notes 77
hegemony 50, 56, 61, 63, 65–75, 118
Helms, Jesse 9
Helms–Burton Act 74, 121
Holbrooke, Richard 136
Hopkins, Harry 21
Hosokawa, Morihiro 112; summit 111
House of Representatives 2, 8
human rights 2–7, 34, 115, 130, 137; Jewish emigration 3
Hungarian Uprising 29, 57, 83, 98
Huntington, Samuel 127
Huntley, James R. 129–130
Hussein, King of Jordan 117
Hussein, Saddam 116

idealism 5–7, 129–131, 134–5, 137
India 81, 86, 110, 118, 122
Inter-Continental Ballistic Missiles 5, 12, 32, 71
Intermediate Nuclear Force 40
Intermediate Nuclear Force Treaty 40
Intermediate Range Ballistic Missiles 70–1
International Monetary Fund 13, 19, 21, 47–8, 108–9
International Trade Organisation 8, 47
internationalism 3–5
interventionism (US) 124–37
Iran 20–1, 28, 37, 51, 95, 97, 99, 105, 115–16, 118; hostage crisis 8, 100, 126; Iran–Contra Affair, 8, 9, 10, 14–15, 43, 69; revolution 100; see also Nicaragua
Iraq 115–118, 122, 133; see also Gulf War
Islamic fundamentalism 91, 104; Ayatollah Khomeini 100
isolationism 3–5, 55
Israel 94–6, 98–103, 116, 118
Italy 52

Jackson–Vanik Amendment 36–7
Japan 20, 22, 27, 34, 49, 52–3, 65, 76–7, 79–80, 85–6, 89, 104, 111–12, 122
Johnson, Lyndon 11, 32–3, 49, 67, 70, 83–4, 98–9
Joint Chiefs of Staff 11

Kampuchea 39
Kantor, Mickey 53–4, 111
Kennan, George 21–5, 34, 94, 102; Long Telegram, 21–2
Kennedy, John 11, 29–33, 39, 49, 61, 70–4, 82–3, 92, 94, 98; Alliance for Progress, 32, 67–8; flexible response 30–3; Grand Design 61; New Frontier 30
Kennedy, Paul 46, 125–6
Kennedy, Robert 72–3
Keynes, John Maynard 50, 52
Kirkpatrick, Jeanne 44
Kissinger, Henry 11, 35–6, 41, 49, 51, 84–5, 99–100; linkage 35
Kohl, Helmut 43
Korea 110, 113; Korean War 14, 24–6,

28, 31, 59, 70, 76, 79–81, 88, 92;
South Korea 8, 24, 27
Kosovo 104, 107, 109–10, 121–2, 128, 136
Krushchev, Nikita 57, 67, 69–73, 86
Kuwait 116

Lake, Anthony 11, 17, 131
Laos 82, 84
Lebanon 39, 97, 101–2, 117; US marine deaths 101
Lend-Lease 18–19
Lesser Developed Countries 51–2
Libya 43, 105; US air strike 101
Limited Nuclear Test Ban Treaty 31, 73
Lincoln, Abraham 15
Lithuania 42
Lundestad, Geir 56

MacArthur, Douglas 25, 79, 81
Macmillan, Harold 61, 82
Magdoff, Harry 50
Maier, Charles 56
Malta Summit (1989) 42
Mao, Zedong 23, 25, 77–8, 80, 86, 88
Marshall, George 10, 77–8; Marshall Plan 22, 48, 56, 58–9, 63;
Organisation for European Economic Co–operation 59
McCarthy, Joseph 10, 14, 23, 76, 78, 80, 88
McNamara, Robert 31, 72
Mearsheimer, John 127–8
Medium Range Ballistic Missiles 70–1
Mercosur 119,
Mexico 53, 119
Middle East 27, 33, 43, 56, 94–104, 106, 115–18; Camp David Accords 100; Madrid Conference 116; peace process 114–118, 122; Resolution 15; US Twin Pillar Strategy 99–101
Milosevic, Slobodan 107, 122, 136
Minh, Ho Chi 80–2, 85
Molotov, Vyacheslav 20–1
Monnet, Jean 59
Monroe Doctrine 3, 119; Corollary 4, 119
Mosadeq, Mohammed 97, 100
Most Favoured Nation 42, 48, 87, 113–14, 122
Multilateral Nuclear Force 61

multilateralism 47–50, 52, 54–5, 61, 112
multinational corporations 1, 51
Mutual Assured Destruction 30, 32, 34–5, 39

Nasser, Gamal Abdul 98
National Economic Council 12, 16, 53
National Security Act 10
National Security Advisor 10, 16; see also list of NSAs
National Security Council 10–14, 16
Nationalist China, see Tawain
neo-realism 6, 127–9, 137
Netanyahu, Binyamin 117
New International Economic Order 50–1
New World Order 12, 34, 41, 105, 121–2, 124, 131, 133; assertive multilateralism 116, 124–5, 129–31, 134; Presidential Directive (25) 122, 130, 135
Nicaragua 66, 74; Contras 39, 68–9; Sandinistas 37, 68–9
Nitze, Paul 23; Committee on the Present Danger 36
Nixon, Richard 10–11,15, 33, 35, 39, 41, 49–50, 62–3, 67, 76, 84–5, 87, 93, 98–101; Doctrine 34; opening to China 35–6
Noriega, Manuel 39, 105, 119–20, 132–3
North American Free Trade Agreement 1, 53–5, 118–19, 137
North Atlantic Treaty Organisation 13, 27, 29, 40, 42–3, 57–9, 61–4, 72, 88, 99, 105–7, 109, 129, 134–6
North, Oliver 15
Nuclear Non-Proliferation and Comprehensive Test Ban Treaties 118, 122
Nye, Joseph 46, 125–6

Okinawa 80, 86, 112
Omnibus Trade and Competitiveness Act 53–4
Organisation of American States 66, 72, 120, 129
Organisation of Arab Petroleum Exporting Countries 100

Apart: The Foundations of United States Policy Toward Latin America, Baltimore, Hopkins University Press, 1990; W. LaFeber, *Inevitable Revolutions: The United States in Central America*, 2nd edit., New York, W.W. Norton, 1993.

For debates about the US role in the post-Cold War world see F. Fukuyama, *The End of History and the Last Man*, London, Hamish Hamilton, 1992; S.P. Huntington, 'The Clash of Civilizations?', *Foreign Affairs*, 1993, vol. 72, pp. 22–49; M. Cox, *US Foreign Policy after the Cold War*, London, Pinter/Royal Institute of International Affairs, 1995; J.R. Huntley, *Pax Democratica: A Strategy for the 21st Century*, Basingstoke, Macmillan, 1998; J. Mearsheimer, 'Back to the Future: Instability in Europe After the Cold War', *International Security*, 1990, vol. 15, pp. 4–57. And for the decline debate, see P. Kennedy, *The Rise and Fall of the Great Powers*, London, Unwin Hyman, 1988; J.S. Nye, *Bound to Lead*, New York, Basic Books, 1991; D.P. Calleo, *Beyond American Hegemony*, New York, Basic Books, 1987; E.N. Luttwack, *The Endangered American Dream*, New York, Simon and Schuster, 1993.

The reader might also wish to consult journals, a selection of which follows: *Diplomatic History*; *Journal of Contemporary History*; *Diplomacy & Statecraft*; *Review of International Studies*; *Journal of Cold War History*; *The International History Review*; *International Security*; *Foreign Affairs*; *Foreign Policy*; *Journal of American History*; *International Organization*; *The American Historical Review*; and *International Affairs*.